INTERNATIONAL TRADE

AN APPLICATION
OF ECONOMIC THEORY

WITH AN EXCERPT FROM
Imperialism,
The Highest Stage Of Capitalism
BY V. I. LENIN

By

J. A. HOBSON

First published in 1904

British Library Cataloguing-in-Publication Data
A catalogue record for this book is available
from the British Library

THE HIGHEST
STAGE OF CAPITALISM

AN EXCERPT FROM
Imperialism,
The Highest Stage Of Capitalism
BY V. I. LENIN

During the past fifteen or twenty years, especially after the Spanish-American War (1898) and the Anglo-Boer War (1899-1902), the economic and also the political literature of the old and new world has more and more often adopted the term "imperialism" in order to characterise the epoch in which we live. In 1902, *Imperialism*, a work by English economist, J. A. Hobson, was published in London and New York. The author, who adopts the point of view of bourgeois social reformism and pacifism, which in essence is identical with the present position of the ex-Marxist, K. Kautsky, gives a very good and detailed description of the principal economic and political characteristics of imperialism.... Hobson, in his work on imperialism, marks the years 1884-1900 as being the period of intensified "expansion" of the chief European states. According to his estimate, England during these years acquired 3.7 million square miles of territory with a population of 57 million ; France acquired 3.6 million ; Germany one million square miles with 16.7 million inhabitants ; Belgium 900,000 square miles with 30 million inhabitants ; Portugal 800,000 square miles with 9 million inhabitants. The quest for colonies by all capitalist states at the end of the nineteenth century, and particularly since the 1880's, is a well-known fact in the history of diplomacy and of foreign policy.

PREFACE

THINKING it possible that some students of fiscal policy may retain sufficient regard for economic principles to seek their aid towards a clearer understanding of the issues involved in International Trade, I have designed in these chapters to make an orderly application of some leading principles to the questions of Free Trade and of Preferential and Protective Tariffs.

My aim has been to use as sparingly as possible the technical language of economic science, and to give so clear an explanation of the terms I use as to enable those unversed in that science to understand the lines of argument. A somewhat close following of the methods of discussion commonly employed by protectionists and free traders alike has impressed me with the urgent need of more rigorous thought, and of a removal of the subject from the heated atmosphere of partisan controversy to one more favourable to a calm and concluded judgment.

PREFACE

The book contains no new theory, but it departs in one important particular from the treatment of international trade adopted in Great Britain by most economic writers since Ricardo and J. S. Mill. This departure consists in a simplification of the theory of foreign trade by the extension to it of the same laws as govern the rates of exchange between commodities within a single nation. This repudiation of the necessity of a separate theory for the determination of international values, if it is accepted, greatly reduces the complexity which, even in so clear and powerful a presentation as that of Professor Bastable, bewilders readers, and which in the treatment by J. S. Mill has led to hopeless entanglement and contradiction.

While limits of space forbid the use of lengthy illustrations, the statement given here claims to be distinctively concrete. It seeks to examine the most vital issues relating to free exchange and tariffs, and to vindicate the rightful authority of economic principles by showing how they explain the actual phenomena of international trade.

I desire to express my thanks to the editor of the *Contemporary Review* for permission to republish an article on "The Mystery of Dumping" and a portion of an article on "The Inner Meaning of

PREFACE

Protection," which appeared in recent issues of that Review, and to the editor of the *Westminster Gazette* for similar permission to embody parts of several shorter articles in chapters of this book.

February, 1904

CONTENTS

CHAPTER IV

NATIONS AS TRADING GROUPS

CHAPTER V

NON-PROTECTIVE IMPORT DUTIES

CHAPTER VI

THE INCIDENCE OF PROTECTIVE AND PREFERENTIAL DUTIES

CHAPTER VII

HOW THE BALANCE OF IMPORTS AND EXPORTS IS ACHIEVED

CHAPTER VIII

WHAT A NATION BUYS AND WHAT IT PAYS WITH

CHAPTER IX

CAN PROTECTIVE COUNTRIES "SUCK" A FREE-TRADE COUNTRY?

CHAPTER X

THE MYSTERY OF "DUMPING"

CHAPTER XI

PROTECTION AS A REMEDY FOR UNEMPLOYMENT

CHAPTER XII

PROTECTION AND SOCIALISM

INTERNATIONAL TRADE

CHAPTER I

THE IMPORTANCE OF EXTERNAL TRADE

§ 1

SINCE the end of industry is to place consumable goods in the hands of consumers, the industrial prosperity of a nation is measured by the quantity of material and non-material goods of various sorts which are consumed by its members. The employment of capital and labour in the industrial arts, trades, and professions is to be regarded as a means to the production of commodities. The quantity of such employment cannot, however, be taken as a reliable index of industrial prosperity, for that country will be most prosperous which can secure through home industry or foreign commerce the largest number and variety of commodities for the smallest employment of capital and labour. Industrial progress, indeed, depends upon the economy of capital and labour. It is of the first importance to the understanding of the nature and uses of commerce to recognise that it

B

must be regarded solely as an instrument for getting commodities into the hands of consumers.

The scientific measurement of industrial prosperity would consist in an assessment of real incomes as expressed in goods and services paid to members of the community in return for the use of some capital or labour-power which they possessed, or as a pension, valued according to some objective or subjective standard of utility. The services here included in real income would comprise all official, professional, domestic, and other personal services bought and paid for by the money income of members of the community. Such services, though generally admitted to be wealth, are usually excluded from considerations of the industrial condition of a nation, and are sometimes excluded from estimates of the national income. But, however convenient for some purposes, this exclusion is quite unjustified. The real income of a nation, as of an individual, must be held to consist of all the utilities, whether embodied in material forms or in human services, which it is able to command. A nation which devotes a larger proportion of its productive energy to increasing the speed and accuracy of the distribution of material goods, or to the better cultivation of the intellectual arts and the provision of professional, artistic, and recreative services, cannot reasonably be regarded as stationary or retrogressive in industrial prosperity. If we describe the money income of the British nation as amounting to £1,700,000,000 per annum, we must regard that money income as represented by a real income consisting partly in consumable material goods consumed during the year, partly in material goods non-consumable which constitute "savings" and form an increase of the forms of capital, and partly in non-material goods which are either consumed as "services" or saved as personal capital, *i.e.* increased power of producing services.

It must be clearly understood that here is no attempt to break down the ordinary limits of wealth and income adopted for the purposes of economic science. We do not include in real income all the intellectual, artistic, and other output which might be loosely regarded as part of the "wealth" of the nation, but only such part as is actually bought and sold.

§ 2. While, therefore, it is allowable and convenient to restrict "industry" for some purposes to the production of material wealth for markets, we cannot apply such restriction in a philosophic consideration of the industrial prosperity of a nation. All forms of non-material wealth which are produced, sold, and consumed by the nation must be regarded as forming part of the real income of the nation equally with food and furniture ; and the energy which goes into the production of this wealth must rank as industrial energy. Unless thinking persons will consent entirely to ignore the old cleavage between material and non-material wealth, and between productive and unproductive services, and to regard as "industrial" all processes which conduce to the production of anything that is bought and sold, it is impossible to form clear judgments about the industrial prosperity of a nation and the part which external trade plays in it.

§ 3. The reason for this insistence becomes evident when we regard the development of needs and satisfactions which mark the history of a progressive nation. In earlier stages of industrial development, progress will consist primarily in the increase of the quantity and variety of material goods for the satisfaction of simple physical wants. Most of the industrial energy of a population in an early stage will go into the extractive arts of agriculture and of certain simple modes of manufacture ; a little later on mining will play a considerable part as an extractive industry, and the modes of manufacture will be more numerous and complex. As industrial civilisation advances under the pressure of expanding needs, a smaller proportion of energy will be devoted to the extractive arts and the primary manufactures, a larger proportion to the more complex industrial processes adapting raw materials or crude manufactures to the more special needs of various classes of consumers. A very rapid increase of population may delay this process by keeping a large proportion of energy employed in raising food ; a very rapid expansion of certain crude sorts of manufacture for foreign trade with less advanced peoples may similarly cause a temporary retardation. But the universal tendency of modern industrial civilisation is to engage a larger proportion of industrial energy in the later and more specialised processes of adapting matter to the satisfaction of a greater variety of special needs. This implies the growth of a qualitative economy of wealth; every further increase of wealth will be attended by a reduction of the increase of raw materials. Still more important will be the increasing proportion of industrial energy engaged in the transport and distributive industries, with the expansion of the area and the complexity of markets which belong to modern industrial civilisation. Finally, a rapidly increasing proportion of energy passes into the production and distribution of non-material wealth, governmental and other public work, professional and personal services, the fine arts, recreation and amusement.

§ 4. The statistics of occupations in every civilised modern nation prove that internal transport, the distributive trades, and professional and other non-material productions are engaging an ever-growing proportion of the national energy; while, as regards production of material forms of wealth, a larger proportion of workers are occupied in the final processes of adapting goods to the special tastes and habits of local groups of consumers. Now this implies that in a normal condition of industrial development a smaller proportion of the real wealth of a nation, *i.e.* of the aggregate of goods and services, is capable of forming the material of international trade.

The actual volume of international trade, and its value, may continue to grow, and the fluctuations in this growth may be matter of serious concern, but external trade will not continue to keep pace with the growth of the wealth of the nation as a whole.

The truth of this generalisation is not impaired by adducing special abnormalities. The external trade of England during the middle decades of the nineteenth century, that of Germany and the United States during the last three decades, may possibly have grown at a more rapid rate than the internal trade and industry, though no proof of such a conjecture is attainable. The sudden quick adoption of new manufacturing methods with new facilities of transport by a few pioneer nations have opened up for them such vast possibilities of profit by trading with the ruck of backward nations as to engage in mining and crude manufacture large masses of industrial energy. Thus for a time the normal tendency may be checked. But since the chief result of the recent preponderating stress on railroad, steamship, and electric development over the whole surface of the globe will be to enable the backward nations to advance more rapidly in agriculture, mining, and manufactures, it is clear that this abnormal importance of the more primitive industrial arts in the life of a few Western nations cannot last. If then it is true that under the recent abnormal circumstances the proportion of the real wealth of such countries as Great Britain, Germany, and the United States, which is suitable for external trade, is diminishing, this diminution will be still greater when the backward countries have learned, as they are learning, to manufacture for themselves. This tendency, as will appear when we consider the nature of international exchange, by no means makes for the disappearance of external trade and the establishment of self-sufficing nations. As industrial civilisation advances, the number, the volume, the value of trades with foreign nations must increase for every civilised nation, but not so fast as the number, the volume, and the values of the internal industry concerned with satisfying wants which are constantly becoming more refined and more largely non-material in their forms.

At the present time it is estimated that between one-fifth and one-sixth of the wage-earners in Great Britain are putting their labour-power into goods for external markets.[1] Since the aggregate income of the working classes (as of the entire nation) is growing far faster than the value of our export trade, it is certain that the proportion of workers who made goods for export was far larger a generation ago, and

[1] Cd., 1761, p. 361.

it is likely it will be far less a generation hence. This simply means that our standard of consumption is being constantly reformed in a direction which makes us less and less dependent upon external goods. Though we shall continue to need increased quantities and new varieties of food, raw materials, and manufactured goods from abroad, they will form a diminishing proportion of the real income of our nation, of the total value of goods and services which we consume.

Setting the same argument in another form, we may say that the poorest classes in Great Britain are in proportion to their incomes the largest consumers of imported goods, chiefly because the largest proportion of their money goes for food; the richest classes are in proportion to their expenditure the smallest consumers of exported goods. Every elevation, then, of the general standard of comfort of the people diminishes the relative importance of external trade and enhances the importance of internal trade.

If, therefore, we found the external trade of Great Britain advancing at a faster rate than the internal trade and furnishing a larger proportion of the aggregate wealth of the nation, we should have grave reason for alarm regarding the industrial progress of the nation.

§ 5. When a civilised nation has, by a sufficient process of investigation of her own resources, as compared with those of other countries, discovered what kinds and amounts of raw materials and commodities she can procure better and cheaper from abroad, and what goods of her own production she can best use to pay for them, and when she has established regular channels of import and export trade in accordance with this knowledge, her further development of external trade will naturally slacken, growing in amount and changing in character with the changes of industrial methods and of habits of consumption, failures of limited natural resources, and the growth or decline of population at home or in the several foreign countries. The swift application of new scientific methods in manufacture, the rapid opening of new large foreign markets, the sudden discovery of hitherto neglected home resources may give a spurt or a temporary boom to external trade. The application of steam and electricity to transport and to manufacture has afforded examples of these abnormal periods of development, and smaller inventions and discoveries will continue to break the regular operation of the economic law, according to which internal industry grows faster than the external trade of nations.

Apart from these changes in the natural resources and industrial arts of nations, there is no reason to suppose that, after a substantially sound division of labour among nations in the growth of food, development of mines, in the cruder forms of manufacture, and a few special lines of commodity where skill and artistic taste play an important part, specialisation of national industry and the trade intercourse it involves should proceed further at any rapid rate. When a nation has once established firm reliable business connections with other nations along these lines of obviously profitable intercourse, a slow growth of external trade is always to be expected. Germany and the United States have in recent years been engaged in establishing lines of enduring intercourse with other nations similar to those which we established in earlier decades of the nineteenth century. Though, in doing so, they may cut across certain of our lines and oblige us to make alterations and readjustments in the character of our external trade, there is no reason to suppose that their external trade will not conform to the same economic law as ours, slackening its rate of growth until it has become as slow as ours. When the main lines of external trade are once laid down, the chief factors making for its increase will be a growth of population and a rise of the cruder standard of comfort of the poorer classes. When population exhibits a declining rate of growth, and when the mass of the population of a country has attained a tolerably large command of material necessaries and conveniences, it is unreasonable to look for a further rapid increase either of the volume or the values of external trade ; industrial progress for the future is contained more and more in the elaboration of internal trade and industry and in the diversion of an ever larger share of energy to the creation and distribution of intangible commodities.

§ 6. The rise and fall of external trade cannot therefore in itself be rightly taken as an index of the industrial prosperity of a nation. Still less can short periods of fluctuation over a few years furnish any evidence of the general condition of trade. A *reductio ad absurdum* of this short-range test has been lately furnished by the statistics of foreign trade of the United States, where an extraordinarily rapid growth of manufacturing export trade suffered a signal collapse during a period of phenomenal prosperity. The explanation was, of course, quite simple. Up to 1900 the development of the new American manufactures, chiefly in the metal trades, was so rapid that, after supplying fully the home market, a large and increasing surplus remained which sought foreign markets. After 1900 the internal enterprise of American industry became for a time so great as to absorb for domestic use the greater part of the former surplus, so that the export trade suffered a great depression.

There are several fairly satisfactory tests of fluctuations in the general industrial condition of a nation. In Great Britain the gross income-tax returns, conjoined with evidence of wage rates in representative trades, furnish such a test, to be fortified by evidence of the consumption of certain kinds of food, and by statistics of banking and insurance. The returns of the railroads, the output and employment of labour in mining and other fundamental industries, are valid evidence of the material prosperity of a country.

Values and volumes of imports and exports taken by themselves are no reliable index of the industrial prosperity of a nation, for there is no fixed law of interdependence between external trade and internal industries even with regard to the production of material wealth: a temporary contraction of internal trade and industry is quite consistent with an expansion of external trade, and *vice versâ*. Of the two trades, import and export, the former, however, is a somewhat truer index of the shorter fluctuations in the material prosperity of a nation than the latter, inasmuch as increasing wealth brought into a country from outside, as food, raw material, or manufactured goods, implies an expansion both of internal industry and of consumption, whereas a temporary increase of exports may imply not an expansion of home industries so large as to overflow more freely into foreign markets, but a positive contraction of home markets. The necessity, however, of a balance between import and export trade in the long run does not justify us in asserting this superiority of import trade as an index of national prosperity excepting for short periodic changes.

CHAPTER II

THE ALPHABET OF FREE EXCHANGE

§ 1

BEFORE entering on a study of the principles of International Exchange, a clear understanding of the economy of exchange between individual members of a single group or commercial society is essential.

It is not difficult to see how liberty of exchange benefits a whole society and each of its members where complete mobility of capital and labour and equal access to natural resources of the land exist. Under such circumstances each owner of industrial energy will be impelled " as by an invisible hand " in pursuit of his own self-interest so to dispose his capital and labour as to contribute to the maximum wealth of society. In other words, free exchange will be the safest guarantee of the most economical division of labour. Let us build up this theory by a concrete illustration, so as to see just where the prime simplicity begins to disappear and difficulties to appear.

A little group of pioneers settles down in a newly opened land along the bank of a creek, cut off from all other society, and compelled to form a self-sufficing community. They bring with them various sorts and degrees of strength, skill, and experience, some having several crafts, others only one, but all willing to turn their hands to any industry which they can most profitably undertake.

A, B, and C will settle down to farming, taking the clearest, most fertile, and convenient land, and will raise food, partly for their own consumption, partly for exchange. D will be a miller and baker, E a smith, F a tailor, G a carpenter, and so on, each undertaking some work for which he has a natural aptitude or some advantage of experience. In order that the division of labour most conducive to the general wealth may be secured, it does not follow that each man will undertake the sort of work in which he is most proficient. A may be the best man all round, capable of making a better miller than D, a better smith than E, and a better carpenter than G, etc.; but, possessing this universal superiority, he selects farming because his relative superiority for that work is greater than for other crafts. D, then, who acts as miller, is not absolutely the best miller, for A is better; indeed, it may also be the case that E, the smith, would have made a better miller than D. But if E had chosen to be miller, either D, a weakly man, must have taken E's place as smith, in which case the community would have lost more by having a bad smith than they gained in a better miller ; or else F, G, or some other person hardly more competent, must have taken the part of smith, D acting as his substitute in the post thus vacated, an arrangement which might have proved equally wasteful as regards the productivity of the community. Evidently it is desirable that each person should undertake, not necessarily that work which he can do better than any other man, or that work which he can do better than any other work, but that work which, if he undertake it, permits the best disposal of the productive powers of the rest of the community.

§ 2. But what force will impel each man to undertake the work which it is best for the community that he should do ? We are not at liberty to assume that any man will sacrifice any private gain he can secure to serve the general good. We can easily understand why A is induced to choose farming, though he would have also made the best smith or carpenter, for we assumed his superiority as farmer to be greater than his superiority as smith or carpenter, so that by taking to farming he will have a larger absolute surplus of goods for exchange against other goods than if he had chosen to be smith or carpenter.

But turn to the case of E, the smith. It may well have been the fact that E would not merely have made a better miller than D, but that he might even have made a somewhat better miller than he made smith in the sense that after satisfying his own needs he would have had a larger surplus-product available for exchange with the products of the others. How is he induced to accept a post which seems less profitable for him than the post of miller? The fact, however, is that, though as miller he might have made a somewhat larger surplus for exchange, his choice of this work would have caused an arrangement of other kinds of work so disadvantageous as to reduce the quantity of other goods which he could get in exchange for his surplus of miller's goods to a smaller amount than he can get for a smaller absolute surplus of smith's goods. So, following his personal gain, he prefers his work of smith. Similarly, all the other members of our group are impelled to choose that work which at once brings them the greatest gain and conduces to the greatest wealth of the group, choosing not always the work they can do best, but the work which it is socially best for them to do.

§ 3. This is a simple statement of the true economy of a *laissez-faire* society. The accurate adjustment of this economy is seen to rest upon the single condition of Free Exchange. Interfere with that at any point or in any degree, and the real income of the community as a whole and of each member is reduced. Suppose, for example, that our miller D, conceiving a dislike for A, charges him a higher price than B or C for grinding his wheat, or exercises a similar preference in exchanging bread for the product of the carpenter, the smith, or the tailor. The effect might be to drive A from farming, where we saw his work was most serviceable to the group, into carpentering or tailoring, where it would be less serviceable. So with any other preference exercised by D or any other person in the terms of exchange. Such preference would injure the aggregate productivity of the group, and each member would suffer.

The recipient of such a preference might seem to gain ; but part of that gain would be offset by a loss he would suffer in his exchange relations with the rest of the injured community. Moreover, such preference here assumed, in order to test its result, is not a valid hypothesis in a society supposed to be actuated by self-seeking motives. For D, or any person, thus venting a grudge or bestowing a favour, is sacrificing his own personal gain, for this discriminative conduct, impairing the general economy, reacts injuriously on him in his exchanges. If the result of his action is to drive A from farming and put E or F in his place, he will have to pay more for grain, owing to the reduced productivity of the farmers.

§ 4. So long as the community is so small that there is not work enough for more than one carpenter,

c

tailor, shoemaker, etc., this economy of Free Exchange works with some considerable friction. It would not be easy to know that the right man was acting as smith, carpenter, or tailor, nor would it be easy to know that he was not exchanging his goods against other goods at a higher rate than he ought. As long as a tailor or a carpenter had a "monopoly" of the trade, he could only be prevented from arbitrarily raising the rate at which he would exchange a coat or a table against flour or other goods by forcing the others to try and make their own coats or tables, or else to do without these conveniences—both of them expensive checks.

Hence, though even in the simplest society, freedom of exchange does conduce to the best economy for all and each, in order to function effectively, direct competition must support the power of substitution. If A were the only wheat grower, he might use his power to exchange his wheat too dearly against coats, boots, or furniture, and so impair the general productivity by forcing D, E, F, etc., either to spend part of their time in cultivating wheat land or to consume less food than formerly, and so to damage their general efficiency. The existence of direct competition between A, B, and C prevents this waste; and since each in his turn gains from the maintenance of the maximum efficiency of the group when he comes to exchange his surplus wheat, the competition or rivalry between these farmers does not prevent our recognising them as co-operative members in the general industrial process.

§5. Next let us suppose the settlement grows more numerous, and some of the farmers decide upon crossing the creek to cultivate land along the other bank. They are accompanied by one or more members of the other trades, and they set up a separate village on the other side. Intercourse is kept up between the villages ; the villages, as villages, do not trade with one another, but the individual villagers do. It evidently remains desirable for each and all that this intercourse should continue quite free. To place a toll upon goods crossing the river because their producers lived on a different side of the stream would evidently be as foolish and as injurious as to put a barrier upon the free intercourse between these same producers when they occupied different streets in the same village.

The real trade is entirely conducted between individual members of this split community, and it is advantageous for each of them to buy and sell most freely on both sides of the stream. If one chooses for any purpose to assess separately the aggregate wealth of each of the two villages, it will be found to be greatest in proportion as this perfect freedom is secured. Any barrier set upon the transport either of persons or goods must, by impairing freedom of exchange, impair the real income obtained through processes of production and exchange for each village and each villager.

§ 6. Next suppose that the village on the other side of the creek set up a separate government of its own, or were annexed by a neighbouring state which claimed sovereignty over the land on that side of the creek, would this fact of political separation affect the utility of preserving the policy of free exchange between the persons living on both sides of the creek? Obviously not. Freedom of exchange would still tend to make each person on either side dispose of his labour-power and his capital in a manner which conduced to the maximum productivity of the two villages, regarded as an economic group; and each villager would continue to get a share of this productivity which would be larger than he could get by any other disposition of economic resources. The political separation of the two villages could not in itself affect the economic gain of maintaining the old relations. Except where political interference with these trade relations is expressly contrived, there is no plausibility in the mistaken notion that villages, towns, or nations engage in trade with one another. In our example it is not the villages which exchange with one another, but individual villagers; and whatever opposition of immediate interests arises in trade intercourse, is more frequent, keener, and more persistent between persons engaged in the same trade in the same village than in the different villages.

What applies to these two villages, politically divided, applies to the entire states of which they form part. No jot or tittle of the economy of Free Exchange is abated by increasing the number of persons on both sides of the stream engaging in commercial inter-course, or by expanding the trade-area. These primary verities and utilities of Free Exchange are nowise affected by the fact that the persons en-gaging in exchange may be gathered into two or more separate groups for purposes of political govern-ment. It is true that the *possibility* of economic self-sufficiency is greater as the group is larger and admits more division of labour; but this does not cancel the damage of erecting barriers. For every extension of the area of free markets secures a more effective division of labour, a larger general production of wealth, and a larger absolute share for each free participant. It is of prime importance to keep in mind the fact that political units are not com-mercial units. Nations do not trade with one another. The notion that they do is falsely suggested by the fact that governments, acting in the real or supposed interest of certain of their citizens grouped in "trades" or "interests," and exercising political influence in order to benefit their private businesses, establish "tariffs" and other politico-economic devices. The practical influence which political boundaries exercise, by limiting the mobility of capital and labour from one state to another, will receive due consideration later on.   At present it must suffice to recognise that the primary advantages of free exchange to a number of farmers, manufacturers, merchants, and others buying and selling in common markets, are nowise affected by the fact that some of them are citizens of Great Britain, others of France or Germany, and others again of the United States.   Free Exchange, whatever the area, and regardless of political boundaries, is the first condition and instrument of that application of industrial energy by all participants, which shall secure the greatest aggregate of wealth and the absolutely largest amount for each member of this industrial commonwealth.

This conclusion is very far from implying that any actual practice of Free Exchange affords a guarantee of a fair and equal distribution of the enlarged product which division of labour secures, either among individuals, trades, or among industrial individuals grouped politically as nations.   It is, indeed, these apparent imperfections in distribution of wealth by so-called Free Exchange that are often made the pretexts of political regulations in the form of Tariffs, Bounties, etc.

CHAPTER III

EXCHANGE BETWEEN "NON-COMPETING GROUPS"

§ 1

IN order to understand the economic impediments in the way of Free Exchange with a view to considering how far the claims of Protectionists and Tariff Reformers to remove them are valid, it is first necessary to study closely the play of the forces which determine the conditions of exchange of goods in our small primitive community.

Let us then return to this split society with several farmers on each side of the creek, and with (say) one tailor, one carpenter, one shoemaker, and one miller in each village.

In such an industrial society in what ratio would commodities exchange with one another, and in what proportion would the advantages of such exchange be divided among the participants? If F, the tailor, puts twice as much time and trouble (*i.e.* cost) into making a coat as H, the shoemaker, puts into making a pair of boots, it is evident that these two commodities exchange in the ratio of two

23

to one. For if F tried to demand three pairs of boots for a coat instead of two, he could not get them. The other tailor across the creek would under-bid him; or H would rather do without a new coat than make an exorbitant exchange; or finally, a handy man himself, he would make a coat for himself. It is easy to see that given free competition, mobility and adaptability of labour-power, a coat and a pair of boots must exchange according to the trouble or cost incurred in making them. And if a coat and boots, then other commodities—a sack of flour, a hatchet, a table—must exchange in proportion to the trouble they respectively cost to make. In the cruder stage of such barter the rate of exchange would be a rough average of this cost, each separate act of exchange being liable to diverge from this "rate" to meet some special case of cost. So, though the rate of exchange between coat and boots might be one coat to two pairs of boots, a shoemaker who had some stock in hand might give three pairs for a coat, if the tailor were very busy and had to work extra time to make the coat. If, however, this was not an accidental situation, but due to an industrial improvement which enabled the shoemaker to produce shoes more easily than before, it is evident that this over-supply of shoes in relation to coats would establish a new ratio in the exchange rate of coats and shoes to accord with a new cost rate.

If the mechanism of barter is somewhat more organised, so that several tailors and several shoe-makers with different degrees of skill and industry are at work, it is quite evident that the rate of exchange between coats and boots will be directly measured by the relation between the "cost" of making the coat made by the slowest tailor at the end of his day's work, and the cost of making the boots made by the least efficient shoemaker under the same circumstances. For if there were complete mobility of labour and equal general aptitude for the two kinds of work, and on account of some increased demand for coats or the sudden death of the best tailor, the day's work of the least efficient tailor purchased more boots and other commodities than before, the next boy who reached working years would take to tailoring, or some shoemaker would take on some tailoring work. It is indeed manifest that any increased or decreased difficulty in buying coats, by paying boots, or flour, or hatchets, will draw industrial energy from the margin of other pursuits into tailoring, or will draw the least productive tailors into some other craft. If an hour's tailoring by a new "hand" is able to exchange its product against a larger quantity of other commodities than an hour's work by a new "hand" at any other craft, it is clear that there will be a set made into tailoring until the level is once more reached. This rate of exchange will not depend upon the relative cost of the most efficient workers in each craft. The most skilful tailor may be able to get twice as much flour in exchange for his day's product as the most skilful shoemaker, provided the least skilful tailor is only able to get the same quantity as the least skilful shoemaker.[1]

§ 2. In other words, given mobility and free exchange goods will exchange according to the "final" or "marginal" cost of production, *i.e.* the cost of the most costly portion of the supply. The exchange of these marginal goods brings the minimum gain to those who make the exchange : the coat which the least efficient tailor makes when he is most tired, exchanges against the two pairs of boots made by the least efficient shoemaker under similar circumstances ; and each of them finds it only just worth while to do the work and make the exchange. The other tailors and shoemakers, however, find it well worth while to make and exchange their goods, and even the least skilful, in exchanging the coats or shoes he makes in the earlier and lighter portion of his day's work, makes a considerable profit by exchange. Such gains appear in the economic textbooks as producers' rents.

They are also consumers' rents, if we now reverse

---

[1] The skill and industry of the superior tailor are not, however, without their due effect as determinants of the marginal cost of tailoring, for where they are great a small number of tailors will be employed, and so the least skilful, or marginal, tailor will be a better tailor than where they are small.

the picture and regard it, not from the "costs" side, but from the "utility" side. For as goods in a "free" market exchange according to their "final" costs, so they likewise exchange according to their "final" utilities. The last and most "costly" coats that are made are those least needed, *i.e.* they furnish the least satisfaction in their use; so with the last and most "costly" shoes; and the utility of the product of the least efficient tailor will equal the utility of the product of the least efficient shoemaker. For, assuming complete mobility and free exchange, it is easy to see that if, owing to some new emergency, the utility of the marginal supply of shoes should come to exceed that of the marginal supply of coats, that fact, causing increased demand for shoes, would enable the least efficient shoemaker to obtain more coats and other goods than before for his shoes, and so new free labour would drift into shoemaking rather than into any other work, until the equality of its marginal utility with that of other crafts was re-established. So, on the basis of complete mobility of labour, the rate of exchange established by barter between different sorts of commodities will accord with the ratio of marginal cost or of marginal utility. Neither cost nor utility can be rightly regarded as the sole cause or determinant of value or exchange rate; the value, or relative importance, of goods for exchange is affected by forces operating either on the cost side or the utility side. But any cause which increases or decreases final cost, also increases or decreases final utility, and conversely any cause which increases or decreases final utility, increases or decreases final cost. They vary directly and proportionately. If tailors, hitherto sewing by hand, get hold of sewing machines, their marginal cost of production falls; it "pays" to produce more coats; this increased supply of coats exchanges at a lower rate for boots and other commodities, and by its consumption supplies less utility. A fall of marginal cost thus automatically, under free exchange, brings about a corresponding fall of marginal utility. Or take the converse case. A loss of cattle, causing a shortage of hides, raises the "cost" of producing shoes, so that it no longer "pays" to make the most "costly" shoes, which were formerly just worth while making; the supply of shoes is less and will exchange at a higher rate for coats and other commodities, the marginal shoes supplying by their consumption a greater utility. So a rise of marginal cost produces a rise of marginal utility.

§ 3. Since rates of exchange are seen to vary either with marginal costs or with marginal utility, it is theoretically a matter of indifference which we take for our notation in processes of exchange. By modern theorists of value, utility is commonly preferred, chiefly for two reasons: first, because, consumption being regarded as the end of industry, utility seems the most direct mode of measurement; secondly, because certain sorts of wealth exist, the

value of which does not appear to vary with "cost."
When a stock of goods is strictly limited by a
natural or artificial scarcity, so that it is not open to
"free" industry to add to the supply, rate of exchange seems to have no direct dependence upon
"cost."

But too much is commonly made of these excep-
tions, which are over-emphasised by a too rigid interpretation of what constitutes a single supply or
"market." When the law of substitution is taken
into proper account, it cannot be contended that the
value of goods whose "scarcity" is most absolute,
e.g. "old masters," is unaffected by the "cost" of
producing other articles which appeal to the same
order of taste. If "cost" be interpreted as the difficulty of adding to supply, it becomes virtually identical with "scarcity," for "scarcity" is governed either
by human inertia or the "niggardliness of nature."

But however preferable utility may be for the
general setting of theories of value, there can be
little hesitation in preferring "cost" for handling the
principles and practices of commercial exchange,
even if we have to give separate treatment to the
case of "monopolies." The main reason of this
preference is a "practical" one, the fact that commerce is more organised as a producer's than as a
consumer's business, and that the more numerous and
changing forces are those which affect directly the
processes of production and the "cost" side of the

equation. Therefore, although it will be necessary in the more intimate discussions of problems of exchange, especially as regards the effects produced by tariffs, to give close attention to the "utility" of goods in the hands of consumers, the general principles of exchange are more easily grasped by approaching them from the "costs" side.

The first of these principles then is, that in a community where full mobility of capital and labour coexists with freedom of exchange, goods will exchange according to the "cost" of producing that portion of the supply of each kind which is produced most expensively. In such a community the enlightened self-interest of the individual members, as we have seen, will likewise so harmonise the interests of the members that each will gain most for himself by doing that work whereby he contributes most to the general wealth.

Under these circumstances the most economical division and co-operation of labour is effected by the instrumentality of free exchange.

§ 4. Since complete mobility of capital and labour is a condition of this economy of energy and harmony of interests, we have next to ask, "How if this mobility be not present?" If by custom, caste-system, or unequal apportionment of natural resources, capital and labour be not free to flow into any industry which seems to afford greater net advantages than other industries, but are virtually fixed in their mode of employment, how will free exchange operate in the formation of productive industry and the distribution of the gains of barter? This is the problem of the economy of exchange between members of "non-competing groups"—to adopt the term to which Professor J. E. Cairnes first gave currency.

Since it will be found that the claim of "scientific tariff-makers" to manipulate international exchange for the benefit of their own nation hinges almost entirely upon the attribution of the economic characteristics of non-competing groups to modern commercial nations, it is important to consider closely the economics of exchange among such groups.

It is quite evident that even in the freest of modern industrial societies the mobility of capital and labour is very imperfect, and the hypothesis of virtually "non-competing groups," if not ultimately valid, is at any rate plausible.

So far as existing forms of capital and labour are concerned, they are specialised in certain kinds of material and human agents incapable of transfer to any other sort of use except at great loss ; and new "fluid" capital and labour is impeded in the free choice of its most profitable use by various inequalities of economic opportunity. Though now capital has greater mobility than labour, many real barriers limit for the ordinary man the area of investment; and many fields to which access is not absolutely forbidden he can only enter upon terms of purchase which prune his profit to a low level for the exclusive benefit of the group of capitalists who have fenced round for themselves this particular preserve. Labour notoriously is more restricted : the ordinary labourer even in England to-day has choice of employment only within a narrow limit, not so much of place (for cheapness of transport has extended the spatial area of his market) as of grade; *the* labour market is broken up into many markets, alike of "skilled" and "unskilled" trades, and a labourer is practically precluded by poverty, lack of education, family associations, etc., from exercising a wide choice; while, once fixed in a trade, he finds it difficult to change into another. Though an English worker to-day has more mobility and wider real choice than his ancestors, much stratification still survives.

§ 5. When in such a society different sorts of goods and services come to be exchanged in elaborate processes of barter, the results of this stratification are very evident. The guarantee, provided by complete mobility of capital and labour, that goods would exchange on a basis of equality of "costs," or human "trouble" of production, no longer exists. If everyone were equally free to be a miller or a shoemaker, we saw that flour and shoes must exchange on terms which gave each man the same reward for his "trouble"; but if milling becomes a close corporation which no man can enter without an expensive education and large capital, there is no security that flour will exchange with shoes upon terms which distribute the gain of barter equally. Or again, if every boy were really free to get education and equip himself for medical work, medical service would exchange for domestic service, or for porterage, upon the basis of a comparison of "final" costs, and the ordinary surgeon might get no more pay *per diem* than the ordinary porter. But so long as the opportunity of equipment for the medical profession is less free than that for ordinary manual work, there is nothing to prevent the average or the marginal doctor getting twice, ten times, or a hundred times more service from the porter who employs him than the service he renders in return, as measured by "cost" or trouble. The fee paid by the porter for medical service may represent fifty units of "cost" as compared with one unit received in return. It is clear that in barter of goods and services between members of different groups in such a society, the goods and services do not exchange in accordance with their final cost, in the sense hitherto accorded to that term.

What does determine the rate of exchange, or value, of different sorts of goods in a society composed of non-competing groups? At first sight two circumstances would seem to have equal weight, the degree of intensity of demand, the degree of scarcity

D

of supply. Two persons confronting one another, each with a monopoly of an absolute necessity of life, could have no basis for bargain, unless it be urged that a perception by each of the equal necessity of obtaining a unit of the supply belonging to the other would determine the rate of exchange on a firm basis of utility, a day's necessary supply of the one commodity exchanging for a day's supply of the other. If for two persons in this situation we substitute two groups, competing only among themselves, and with the same aggregate surplus of the two necessaries available for exchange, it is clear that, since *ex hypothesi* each act of exchange has the same importance for one party as for the other, the exchange will again be on a basis of equal utility, with no reference to respective costs. If, however, the intensity of demand is greater for one of the commodities than for the other, the one being a physical necessity, the other only a prime convenience of life, or if, on the other hand, both being necessary, the available surplus of the one was greater than that of the other, it is clear that the commodity to whose demand the greater necessity, or to whose supply the greater scarcity attached, would have a higher rate of exchange than where the conditions were equal. But though it here seems as if intensity of demand played an equal part with scarcity of supply in determining rate of exchange, it can easily be shown that this is not the case. For if the surplus constantly available

for barter in each group exceeded the amount necessary to supply the members of the other group, the
fact that these groups were non-competing would not
prevent the rate of exchange from conforming to the
ordinary rule of free commercial societies: the goods
would exchange according to final costs. The fact
that one class of goods was a necessity, the other only
a convenience, would not give an advantage to the
former. If I am about to purchase a loaf of bread
and a hat under terms of free competition, though the
intensity of my demand for bread *per se* is greater
than that for a hat *per se*, where competing bakers
possess an ample supply of bread the importance of
my obtaining any particular loaf is no greater than
the importance of my obtaining any particular hat;
or in other words, the existence of a competing surplus
supply cancels the influence of intensity of demand in
determining price or rate of exchange.

Though a baker's monopoly is in a stronger bargaining position than a hatter's monopoly, under free competition a baker has no advantage over a hatter on
account of the greater necessity of bread.

It is relative scarcity that determines the strength
of bargain in a society of non-competing groups. If
the hatting trade can keep hats more scarce than the
baking trade can keep loaves, hats will exchange
against loaves at a premium per unit of final cost of
production, *i.e.* the least efficient hatter will make more
than the least efficient baker.

If we are to master the theory of exchange between non-competing groups, we must pay chief regard to the factor of scarcity of supply, and regard intensity or elasticity of demand in its bearing on scarcity. Only in proportion as the non-competing character of groups is reflected in scarcity of supply can it cancel or modify the law of exchange according to final costs. For while immobility of capital and labour between the groups, by limiting competition, impairs the full economy of division of labour and lessens the aggregate productivity of wealth in a community, it does not necessarily affect the rate of exchange between goods and services of different sorts. If an equally rigorous industrial caste system were applicable to all trades, there is no reason why final costs of production should not form an accurate standard of rates of exchange. It is because this immobility is not equally applicable to all trades that rates of exchange diverge from this standard. When access is more difficult to one trade than to another, that greater difficulty will be attended by a corresponding limitation of the freedom of supply of commodities, and this relative scarcity will be a source of gain when this class of goods is bartered against other classes where supply is not thus restricted.

This is of course universally recognised in the case of "monopolies," natural or acquired; final expense of production there forms only the lower limit of a price which is determined by calculating the effect of different fixed quantities of supply upon elasticity of demand, and so ascertaining the degree of scarcity it is desirable to maintain. Maintaining an artificial scarcity is the only mode of enabling a class of goods to exchange against other classes at a higher rate per unit of final cost of production. Where among the members of a "non-competing" group there is such internal rivalry and such large access to raw material and other factors of production as to maintain free competition, no scarcity arises which enables the rate of exchange for this class of goods to rise above the limit set by equality of final costs.

§6. Thus we perceive that the real question of exchange among members of non-competing groups is one of the value of monopoly or scarcity goods. The only light thrown upon the case by the theory of "non-competing groups" is that it gives a more elastic meaning to monopoly prices, enabling us to see that monopoly or scarcity value is not confined to a few instances of close markets, but attaches in different degrees to all markets, or more strictly, to one of the two parties in all markets. Whereas the Standard Oil Company can at the present time fix a rate of exchange for oil (say) 50 per cent. above that which final cost of production would assign to it as compared with commodities in general, a local baker acting in loose collusion with his fellows can charge a premium of (say) 20 per cent. above cost for the bread he sells, while a lawyer by a scarcity partly kept up by his trade union, partly by superior opportunities of education, etc., can get a premium of (say) 80 per cent. in selling his legal advice.

It is quite evident that everywhere both current market and normal prices are affected in widely different degrees by various causes which operate through artificial scarcity of supply. The general rate of exchange in a commercial society is a reflex of these different degrees of scarcity acting on a background of equality of final costs.

§ 7. This enhancement of exchange value over final costs[1] is sometimes termed "rent," where it is a normal or fairly permanent factor. It contains the two essential notes of economic rent: first, it is a surplus above costs, or in other words, forms no necessary inducement to any owner of power of production to apply that power; secondly, if it can be directly "taxed" it has no power to shift the tax.

It should be understood that "monopoly" in the strict sense of single-ownership of supply is by no means essential to maintain a class of goods at an exchange value in excess of final cost. There may be free competition of many owners of supply, but if the trade is fenced against the intrusion of outside capital

---

[1] Where the term "costs" is expressed in money I shall signify by "final" or "marginal costs," not the so-called expenses of production of the marginal product, which often contain elements of scarcity price for some factors of production, but the monetary equivalent of subjective "cost" or "sacrifice" in production.

and labour, the marginal supply may exchange at a premium against other classes of goods produced in trades which capital and labour can enter more freely.

The plainest instance of this process is where an absolutely limited natural supply of some necessary of life is in the possession of a group of persons who have exclusive ownership.

The owners of a strictly limited amount of surface or subsoil of land get as the exchange value of a unit of this land-use an amount of other goods, which has no assignable relation to any " cost" in the shape of expenditure of capital and labour that may have gone into the development of the land. The marginal land has a value measured entirely by its scarcity, and rises or falls as intensity of demand gives increased or diminished importance to this particular sort of scarcity. But wherever privilege, reputation, secret processes, patents, training and special knowledge of markets secure any group of producers against the easy entrance of outside competition, it is quite evident that they possess a power similar to that of landowners to maintain a rate of prices which measures their immunity and is maintained by a restriction of supply. This restriction may not be due to any agreement among the producers, but may arise merely from inability of outside capital and labour to enter in so as to force down marginal prices to a level of equal costs with other trades. But, of course, where such conditions of restricted competition exist, it is common for the beneficiaries to fortify themselves by agreement in the maintenance of a most profitable degree of scarcity, raising prices by deliberate limitation of output, and organising a more vigorous defence against the intrusion of outside competition.

What capitalist employers do workmen also do, so far as they are able, fencing a skilled labour market against outside labour, in order to enable their services to exchange against other goods and services at a rate which exceeds the marginal costs.

This condition of affairs in a trade or a labour market does not, of course, imply that every business in the trade is making profits above the average, every workman a wage above the average. What it does imply is that a given unit of goods or service is exchanging against other unprotected or less protected goods or services at an advantage. An incompetent employer may fail to make both ends meet, although he shares the advantage of selling goods at a premium; by slackness or other inefficiency he may not make enough of the right kinds of goods at the right times for the right markets. So likewise the fact that some doctors or some plasterers may be only making a starvation income is quite consistent with the statement that medical service or plastering commands a scarcity value in exchange against goods and services in general.

§ 8. When due consideration is given to the actual structure of industry, it is evident that where exchange takes place between the goods and services produced by members of "non-competing groups," the competition within each group is not such as to secure that the marginal portion of supply, which regulates the value and the price, is produced under conditions which equalise the costs for the several commodities which are the objects of exchange. Many goods and services thus exchange against other goods at a premium which measures the degree of exclusion conveyed in their "non-competing" character. Whereas the rigid theory of free competition would force goods to exchange according to the human costs or sacrifices involved in producing the marginal portion of supply, the restricted competition which prevails adds to the expenses which represent these costs, other expenses which are scarcity gains or "rents."

A rigorous application of the doctrine of equal marginal costs, for example, might yield the following rates of exchange :—

Butter. Pounds.	Wheat. Bushels.	Coats.	Whisky. Gallons.	Porterage. Hours.	Medical service. Hours.
100	60	3	20	120	150

But the actual rate of exchange on a basis of "non-competing groups" might be as follows :—

Butter. Pounds.	Wheat. Bushels.	Coats.	Whisky. Gallons.	Porterage. Hours.	Medical service. Hours.
100	40	2	14	250	10

The comparative exclusiveness of the several trades operating on scarcity of supply will determine the divergence from the equal costs ratio.

§ 9. Now reflection on the nature of these premiums will show that they are not "quasi-rents" (as they are sometimes termed), but real rents, in the sense that they constitute surpluses over and above the necessary costs and expenses of production, and that they cannot evade the incidence of a direct tax imposed upon them.

In theory it would be possible to devise, in the interests of the whole society constituted by these non-competing groups, a scientific system of direct taxation which, by taking the whole of these scarcity gains or "rents," should remove the entire motive of exclusiveness, so far as it was artificial; and using the taxes to secure equality of opportunity for the entire body of citizens, should re-establish the ratio of exchange upon its natural footing and secure the full, free flow of capital and labour conducive to the maximum productivity of the community.

This theory of taxation of "rents" in order to furnish a public income to be expended in providing equality of opportunity through free education, cheap transit, and other public services, underlies our modern progressive policy of social reform. The theoretical and practical conditions of its success require, however, to be carefully observed.

The first condition is, that if a tax is imposed

either upon a commodity produced under conditions of "scarcity," or upon incomes derived from such a trade or profession, it must be imposed upon all the businesses or persons contributing to the supply of the commodity. If, for instance, there were two or more non-competing groups contributing to the same supply (closed so far as flow of capital and labour was concerned, and only competing in the sale of commodities), a tax imposed upon the product of one group, or upon the incomes of one group, would only strengthen the scarcity or monopoly power of the other group, and would not remove the surplus value or premium enjoyed by the commodity in the processes of exchange. Nor would it throw open the industry to the free flow of capital and labour. If, for example, a tax were imposed upon the cheques or other bank money of joint-stock banks from which private banks were exempt, or *vice versâ*, it is plain that any scarcity gains or "rents" derived from the profitable exclusiveness of the banking business would not disappear under this unfair and unprofitable discrimination. Again, in applying such a theory of taxation, the law of substitution would have to be taken into due account. A tax directed to secure the surplus profits of gas works would, of course, be frustrated in large measure if oil were not subject to a similar tax. Unless the capitalistic structure of these industries was built absolutely water-tight, so that the unequal condition of the two did not draw any capital into the one which otherwise would have been invested in the other, it is plain that the object of the tax will be progressively defeated, and that one industry will be favoured at the expense of another, and to the detriment of the public, which will be confronted by one tighter instead of two looser "monopolies," or "restricted trades." The closer one goes into the physiology of industry, the wider and more intricate become the applications of the law of substitution, the more intricate the inter-action of what at first sight seem separate supplies or "markets."

Thus the theory that the scarcity gains of special trades, regarded as relatively non-competing groups, can be safely and profitably taken by specific measures of taxation, becomes less and less tenable as the basis of a fiscal policy.

In a few large instances where natural limitations operate, as in the case of land values, or legally conferred privileges, as in banking, brewing, and perhaps certain "protected" professions, it may be safe and profitable to direct a special tax at a particular class of commodities, or at the trades which produce them; but the general tendency of rational fiscal policy is likely to go more in the direction of increased taxation of large incomes or large properties, irrespective of their particular origins or uses.

CHAPTER IV

NATIONS AS TRADING GROUPS

§ 1

THE analysis of our last chapter may appear at first sight remote from the issues of international exchange. But in reality the principles and policy towards which we have been working are of direct and tolerably obvious application to this wider sphere.

For it is only in so far as nations constitute non-competing groups, between which there is not free flow of capital and labour, that special problems of international fiscal policy arise. If the trading relations between members of two or more nations were such that capital and labour were free to flow from one nation into any industry of the other nation, the mere fact of a political distinction would not, of course, prevent such a distribution of industrial energy from taking place as would form the basis of an equal exchange of commodities between industries in the two countries. If one of the nations possessed a monopoly or a superiority of soil or other natural resources, limited in extent, which enabled some commodity wanted by both nations to be produced exclusively in one, even this fact, though it would give rise to economic rents paid to the owners of the soil, would not enable the capital and labour engaged therein to enjoy any special gain in the value or rate of exchange between this class of commodities and others freely produced by both nations. How far this "natural monopoly" can be made amenable to a tax on imports we will consider presently. Just now we are concerned to mark the limits of the application of the theory of non-competing groups.

The general disposition of economists who have confronted the question is to assume that the theory will have more stringent application to the conditions of international trade than to inter-group trade within the several nations. They base this view apparently on the belief that capital and labour are less impeded in their flow between the several occupations in the same country than in their flow between similar occupations in different countries.

Now it is very doubtful whether, or how far, this assumption is warrantable. It is a commonplace that capital is becoming cosmopolitan, that is to say, it flows with great freedom over national barriers into large fields of investment, not merely into public loans and into railroad and other public or semi-public occupations, but into a great variety of agricultural, manufacturing, and commercial businesses conducted for profit. Of course, this cosmopolitanism as yet applies to a small proportion of the whole area of investment, even as between Great Britain and the United States, where the stream is freest ; but when one takes into consideration the present condition of such countries as the Transvaal, Argentina, and Chili, it is clear that the barriers of nationality are visibly breaking down so far as certain occupations of capital are concerned. The cosmopolitanisation of labour, so far as certain large labour markets are concerned, does not lag far behind. The spread of knowledge and the facilities of modern carriage have greatly abated the force of Adam Smith's dictum that "man is of all baggage the most difficult of transport." Common or unskilled male labour has acquired immensely increased mobility within the last three decades. Such widely diverse peoples as Irish, Scandinavians, Slavs, Italians, Germans, Malays, Chinese, have exhibited so keen a capacity of migration as largely to equalise over considerable tracts of the earth the conditions of the low-skilled labour market. There are even certain skilled trades, such as mining and engineering, in which national boundaries present few obstacles. The effective class boundaries separating the professional, shopkeeping, mechanic, and labouring classes are perhaps in most of the advanced industrial nations quite as difficult to cross as the national boundaries separating workers in the same trade or handicraft. A Welsh miner or an English engine-driver finds it far easier to earn a livelihood in his own craft in the United States or South America than to enter a profession or a commercial career in Great Britain ; a German clerk can more easily get employment in England, France, or America than become a lawyer or a farmer in Germany; Swiss waiters, Scotch gardeners, English coachmen, Italian cooks, German musicians, Jewish pedlars—to quote a few salient examples—have a capacity to change their country far exceeding their ability to change their occupation in their own country. Even if we direct our attention to young labour just entering the labour market, it is becoming easier to gain employment either in some field of unskilled work or along the lines of some special aptitude in a foreign land than to enter an employment far removed in economic character or social position in one's native country. So far as the older European countries are concerned, the transferability of either capital or labour among them is as yet very slight, affecting a very little proportion of the whole field of production ; but the new world of North and South America, South Africa, and Australasia, and some backward parts of the old world, now submitted to swift development, form huge areas of cosmopolitan industry. These countries can in no wise be regarded as "non-competing groups" in the old sense of exclusive nationalities, and they are becoming larger factors in world-industry each decade. A

common meeting-ground for Europeans of all
nations, they are acting to a quite perceptible extent
as equalisers of the economic conditions of the European nations. Though there is no appreciable direct
flow of agricultural and other manual labour between
Great Britain, Germany, Italy, and Russia, the
common tide of migration into American countries
exercises a marked tendency to raise the economic
conditions of the more backward European nations
to the level of the more forward ones. The growing
size of this indirect competition considerably quali-
fies the application of the theory of " non-competing
groups " to nations which show little transferability
of capital and labour among themselves.

§ 2. Moreover, it must be remembered that we are
concerned with the question of the extent to which
nations are " non-competing groups," not on its own
account, but for its bearing on the question of the
terms upon which goods will be exchanged between
members of these " non-competing groups." If the
non-competing character be so strongly marked in
respect of certain nations, and certain classes of
goods they sell, as to enable these goods to exchange
at a high premium over equal final costs as compared
with other goods of other nations, it seems theoretically possible to devise a scientific tariff to assist
those exchanging at a disadvantage to recoup themselves. If, in other words, Germany, France, United
States, or Russia, are selling us goods artificially

E

enhanced in value by the inclusion of economic rents or high profits, which rest either on natural or contrived scarcity of supply, it is arguable that, by placing a suitable tax on such goods, we might secure for our treasury and so for our nation the whole or part of this rent or surplus value, thus altering the terms of the national exchange to our advantage.

How curiously remote this consideration is from the ordinary conception of the tariff problem appears from the fact that such a proposed tax would be directed against " the foreigner " on the ground that he is selling goods too dear, whereas the zest of our tariff reformers is all directed against him for selling goods too cheap.

Now since cheapness in imports means two things, first, that the foreigner is giving us more than he gets ; second, that the industries which furnish the cheap goods cannot bear a duty and will therefore shift it on to us, the proposal to retaliate by duties on cheap imports is one of palpable folly. The case of selling cheap for a time in order to sell dearer later, which is one of the charges against "dumping" nations, deserves separate consideration ; the real injury committed in such a case would consist not in the temporary cheapness, but in the subsequent preponderating dearness. The only bearing of the theory of " non-competing groups " on international trade has reference to the dearness it imputes to certain classes of imports or exports. Are the restraints upon mobility of capital and labour between nations such as to enable certain groups of exporters in foreign nations to raise abnormally the value of articles we find it necessary to take from them in exchange for the goods we send them? Are they able, by means of monopoly of natural resources, or by legal restraints or social interferences which limit production or commerce, to pay us small quantities of dear goods, taking from us in return large quantities of cheap goods, "dear" and "cheap" having reference to the presence and absence of a surplus over the necessary economic cost of production?

It is, of course, quite conceivable that we might be so dependent upon a commodity of necessity or prime convenience produced abroad by a "non-competing group" that the price might be exorbitantly raised to us. The price we pay the Standard Oil Company for our oil may stand considerably higher than marginal cost of production, limited as it is only by considerations of elasticity of demand in view of the law of substitution. A cornering of our principal wheat supply, now in the United States, later, perhaps, in Canada, may raise the rate of exchange for wheat against our commodities indefinitely high. The real tariff problem has reference to these and similar cases of monopoly, and the practical possibility of devising means for altering the balance of exchange which is against us to one in our favour. It is where national boundaries and national policy serve to raise artificially the value of goods we desire to import that taxation, in economic theory at any rate, may furnish a remedy.

§ 3. Goods produced by foreign nations, cheaply, under freely competitive conditions, obviously make for our advantage in the process of international exchange. Now Great Britain is in this position, that a larger proportion of her imports are produced by industries employing cheap labour and competitive capital than is the case with other nations. The food and raw materials, which constitute the bulk of British imports, are grown under conditions which keep the price close to a competitive marginal cost: a very small proportion of them, such as rubber, diamonds, special qualities of wine, tea, tobacco, lending themselves to any considerable enhancement of values. Similarly, most of the manufactured imports into Great Britain are cheap products of competing foreign industries. This indeed is the head and front of their offending.

Thus it appears that the fact that nations are in large measure "non-competing groups," in the sense that capital and labour do not flow freely between them, is not to any great extent a source of scarcity values for purposes of international trade, so far at any rate as Great Britain is concerned. For the scarcity values which arise in nations trading with us are mostly confined to goods and services destined for internal rather than for external trade.

This was not always so, nor is it so now equally in

all sorts of foreign trade. The earlier international trade consisted chiefly in exchange of articles which were the peculiar products of the respective countries based on some advantage of natural resources, secret process, skill, or custom. Such was the early trade of Eastern, and later of Western Europe with the East—spices, gems, costly cloths, exchanging for silver, tin, copper, slaves, etc. The opening up of world markets by modern facilities of transport has, however, transformed the character of international commerce. It has destroyed the monopoly of single nations in the sale of rare commodities, by opening several alternative sources of supply ; still more important, by cheapening and quickening transport it has enabled great masses of foods, raw materials, and manufactured goods to pass from one nation to another, not because the latter nation could not produce them, but because it could not produce them so advantageously. Every extension and cheapening of transport increases the part played in international trade by common products and reduces the part played by uncommon products.

So whereas in earlier trade natural scarcity and special skill characterised a large part of the articles of international exchange, most modern imports and exports are produced under competitive conditions, which keep down profits and wages to a low level. Though there may be considerable differences in the profits and real wages of those who supply our imports of wheat, sugar, and hides, in various countries, those differences, expressed as differences of cost, will be far less than in the case of rare special products ; and what is even more significant, they will be far less than the differences between their marginal costs and those of other classes of commodities and services in their own country.

Taking the general current of international trade, we find it consisting more and more largely of common articles from the production of which elements of scarcity, and therefore of monopoly-gain, are excluded. Barter of such articles, as we have seen, tends to take place on a basis of equality of marginal costs. When groups of producers in several nations contribute to the market for various common classes of commodities in international exchange, the mere fact that capital and labour does not flow from one nation to another will not prevent the competition of the market from tending to equalise the final costs in the several competing countries. Where, as is now the case, certain "new" countries are drawing capital and labour from other countries which do not freely exchange capital and labour with one another, these former tend sensibly to equalise the conditions of international exchange among the latter.

§ 4. Thus we may conclude that a large and increasing proportion of international trade consists in the barter of goods produced under conditions of tolerably free competition in the country of their origin, and prevented further from exchanging at a premium by the fact that several nations are contributing to each supply.

The inequality of exchanges based on the theory and practice of "non-competing groups" is thus seen to be a far more potent factor in internal than in external trade. Far more injury is done to the economical division of labour by artificial restrictions of the flow of capital and labour within the several nations than by restraints on the international flow, and far larger inequalities are produced in the terms of internal exchange of goods and services by the former restraints than in the terms of external exchange by the latter.

There is therefore a *primâ facie* justification for the view of Socialists and radical social reformers that proposals to redress, by tariffs or other public instruments, the terms of international exchange are designed in the defence of the group-interests which wield a power to extract surplus gains in processes of domestic exchange. In particular, the gravest inequality of exchange in internal trade, where common forms of manual labour-power are exchanged against finished goods and services which contain large elements of scarcity-value, though not absent from international exchange of commodities, is reduced there to a minimum by reason of the universal prevalence of forces tending to keep down

in almost every country the remuneration of the
lower sorts of labour-power to a level of bare
subsistence and low-grade efficiency.

§ 5. We thus reach the conclusion that the theory
of international exchange is not rightly based on
the assumption that nations are " non-competing
groups," and that the ratios of exchange between
their members are therefore generally determined by
the laws of exchange between owners of monopoly
or scarcity goods.   The general law of international
exchange will conform rather to the conditions of
free exchange between competing individuals and
groups, the ratio of exchange being determined by
the relative marginal expenses of production of the
respective commodities.   The general applicability
of this law is not appreciably impaired by the fact
that standards of real wages and of other expenses
of production may differ considerably in the various
countries whose members engage in competition and
exchange.

Modern world-tendencies continually make towards an international exchange based more upon
comparison of final expenses of production and less
upon conditions of monopoly or scarcity,[1] as the
following summary will indicate :—

(*a*) Direct mobility of capital and (to a less ex-

---

[1] The growth of Trusts and other "combines" in the export trade
of some countries must at present be regarded merely as qualifying,
not as reversing, the more general trend of forces.

tent) of labour between different nations for large capitalist enterprises is increasing.

(*b*) An increasing number of nations which are cosmopolitan as regards capital and labour are entering the field of modern industry.

(*c*) The cosmopolitanisation of inventions and industrial methods tends to equalise expenses of production in different nations, and so, by increasing the number of competing "nations" in the various markets, to establish international exchange according to the ratio of marginal costs independently of the direct flow of capital and labour between the several nations.

(*d*) Substitution, or a wider choice of materials and methods in processes of production, and in materials and methods of consumption (the result of an increased exploitation of the materials and forces of nature and a more intelligent rationale of consumption) reduces the economic strength of monopoly or scarcity.

These considerations justify the theoretic treatment of international exchange in accordance with the laws which regulate ordinary cases of exchange among members of a competitive society. As in the latter, so in the former, a number of cases where the conditions of monopoly or scarcity are dominant must be reserved for special treatment.

APPENDIX TO CHAPTER IV.

This application to international exchange of the same laws as apply to individual exchange is of course opposed to the general practice of economists, who have followed Mill's contention that "the value of a thing in any place depends on the cost of its acquisition in that place; which, in the case of an imported article, means the cost of production of the thing which is exported to pay for it" (Book III. chap. xviii. § 1). This, sometimes spoken of as "the first law of international values," is not a law at all. To say that "the value" of an imported article means the cost of production of the thing exported to pay for it merely affirms that the value of the foreign article is equal to (or signifies) the article exported as its equivalent. What we desire to know is, "What determines the *quantum* of the export goods we pay with?" Mill's statement affords no assistance in answering this question, as, indeed, he admits a little later: "The value, then, in any country, of a foreign commodity, depends on the quantity of home produce which must be given to the foreign country in exchange for it. *In other words, the values of foreign commodities depend on the terms of international exchange.*"

So early in his analysis does Mill collapse into sheer tautology. He then admits the "embarrassment" and expresses his intention to "fall back upon an antecedent law, that of supply and demand." But it soon appears that he has no such antecedent law at his disposal, for he proceeds to formulate a law based exclusively on "demand," reverting to a one-sided "utility" theory of international value to balance the equally one-sided "cost" theory which he applied to ordinary processes of exchange. "When two countries trade together in two commodities, the exchange-value of these commodities, relatively to one another, will adjust itself to the inclinations and circumstances of the consumers on both sides." The illustrations by which he seeks to fasten this principle on the mind of his readers assume, not merely that the two countries are absolutely "non-competing groups," but that there is absolute rigidity both in supply and demand on both sides. Even then the law does not carry him very far, for he recognises "that several different rates of international value may all equally fulfil the conditions of this law" (§ 6), and in fact the actual limits within which the rate of exchange will vary are limits set by costs, and not by utility acting on demand. "We know that the limits within which the variation is confined are the ratio between their costs of production in the one country and the ratio between their costs of production in the other" (§ 2). What Mill does recognise, when he is confronted with International Exchange, is that his general law of Value as previously formulated is defective, when applied to cases of monopoly in scarcity of supply. In such cases value appears to depend entirely on the demand side, because supply being *ex hypothesi* fixed, all changes of value are directly the products of changes in effective demand.

So far as Mill's reasoning is valid, it has no special applicability to international trade, but to monopoly or scarcity values in general. The assumption that international trade, either wholly or for the most part, falls under this head is, we find reason to believe, invalid.

CHAPTER V

NON-PROTECTIVE IMPORT DUTIES

§ 1

WHILE the main current of international exchange flows so as fairly to equalise the gains of barter, cases evidently arise where, in theory at any rate, it is possible for a nation, by a policy of import or export duties, to turn the balance of trade to the advantage of its members. Where a nation contains an industry which possesses a natural monopoly, or some great advantage in production controlled by a group of businesses which do not compete freely with one another, it can export this class of goods at an advantage into countries which possess no similar advantages in producing articles for export. The extent of this scarcity gain will seem to depend on the two conditions which determine all values, scarcity (dependent on "costs" or natural limitations) and utility. If such article of export is kept very scarce, and the marginal utility of this limited supply is very great, it enjoys a great advantage in international exchange. But such advantage is not absolute. For if the country receiving such a commodity can oblige the country exporting it to receive payment in imports which enjoy a similar scarcity value, neither nation can be said to enjoy an advantage over the other. If Cape Colony exchanges diamonds for the Standard Oil of the United States, there is no presumption that either country gets the advantage of the other. For if De Beers has a closer control of the output in price of diamonds than the Standard Oil Trust has of oil and its substitutes, the balance is perhaps redressed by the fact that oil represents a more urgent need than diamonds, and so the sale can be extended with less chance of spoiling the market. We are, however, not entitled to assume that America can only send oil to Cape Colony on condition of receiving diamonds in return. The question, "What determines the goods we buy and the goods we pay with?" has not yet been put and answered. We must therefore take the case of a country exporting goods produced at an advantage to a country from which it receives goods produced at no such advantage, and ask what power, if any, the latter possesses to redress the balance.

§ 2. We will first assume, not only that the foreigners possess an advantage in production, but that for export purposes, at any rate, they act in unison, fixing a monopoly price for their goods. The case, in fact, is that of a trust or combination using its power, not to "dump" cheap goods, but to fix prices for exported goods which give a premium on the margin or most expensively produced portion of its supply. If the Standard Oil Trust can place oil in the British market at 6*d.* a gallon, whereas no other adequate supply is available at that price, it need not supply oil at 6*d.*, but may place the price considerably higher, holding in reserve the power to break any outside competition which may intercede by lowering the price to 6*d.* or even less. Thus, endowed with a virtual monopoly of the British market, it may fix the price at 8*d.*, calculating that the aggregate of sales at that price will yield the largest net profit on the trade. This price will be fixed by reference to the marginal expenses of production, which will probably be lower per gallon as the output is increased, and to the urgency of the demand, *i.e.* the effect of a higher price in checking purchases. Here is a scarcity element of 33⅓ per cent. added to the normal price as measured against British goods produced under freely competitive conditions. £75 worth of American oil is able to bloat itself out to the value of £100, and to require £100 worth of (*ex hypothesi*) freely produced British goods to go out in payment. It appears feasible *primâ facie* for Great Britain to impose an import duty up to 33⅓ per cent. *ad valorem* on American oil, obliging the producer to pay the whole of it. Since a normal profit would be made upon every part of this supply entering the market at 6*d.*, it seems as if the British

Government might take 2*d*. per gallon *en route*, leaving the oil to sell at 8*d*. as before, relieving the consuming public in its capacity as taxpayer at the expense of the foreigner. This, indeed, might possibly be done. It might not pay the Standard Oil Trust to endeavour to recoup itself for the payment of the tax by raising the price of oil; for the result of such a rise of price, by diminishing the sales on the one hand, and raising the marginal expenses of production through lessening the output on the other hand, might be a reduction of aggregate profit as compared with the profit derived from maintaining the selling price at 8*d*. But though the foreigner in this situation might pay all the tax, there is no certainty that he would do so. If the monopoly is of a necessary or a prime convenience, as is here the case, a slight rise of price is likely to cause a less than corresponding shrinkage of demand, so that it will generally pay the monopolist to sell a slightly smaller quantity at an enhanced price, the *ad valorem* duty on the enhanced price thus forming a reduced tax on the profit of each unit of the product. The only really scientific tax on a monopoly is one directly imposed, not on the selling price, but on the monopoly element in that price, or, what comes to the same thing, on the surplus profit of the business over the normal return on competitive capital. As I have argued elsewhere,[1] " since we could not presume the monopoly rent to

---

[1] *The Economics of Distribution*, p. 321. (Macmillan and Co.)

vary directly and proportionately with the selling price, an *ad valorem* tax upon selling prices might make it more profitable for a monopolist to restrict production and raise prices."

A really scientific tax upon such a monopoly can only be imposed by the government of the nation in which the income of the monopoly is earned; but it is possible that an import duty might be devised so as to take a large part of the surplus profit. This is a case where detailed consideration of concrete circumstances rightly determines a policy.

If it were tolerably certain that a rise in the price of oil to 9*d.* or 10*d.* would very greatly reduce the sale, and would probably bring other sources of supply or other illuminants into effective competition, it might be a sound fiscal policy to impose the tax. The delicacy, however, of calculating the reaction of a rise of price upon demand on the one hand, and cost of production on the other, would be so great, that taxation of this kind could not be regarded as "scientific," and must always remain speculative.

The case of a "monopoly" of this order is, however, one where it can fairly be argued that a tax will tend to fall in large part on the producer.[1]

§ 3. But, as Mill recognised, it is not necessary to assume "monopoly" in order to get the condition of

---

[1] Mill, however, is not justified in asserting out of hand that "the price cannot be further raised to compensate the tax."

scarcity value for a class of imports. A natural limit of supply may keep prices high, though there may be competing owners of the supply. The familiar instance is that of rare wines, which, though there may be several competing growers, will fetch a price embodying scarcity rent. An import duty on such wine will fall largely on the growers, or more strictly, on the owners of the vineyards. But even here we cannot speak with absolute assurance. The tax must fall wholly on the producers on condition that the market of the taxing country is their only market, and that they cannot raise their price within the taxing country without causing something like a proportionate shrinkage in their sales. Both these are practical considerations which would require to be taken into account if a new tax upon high-priced wines were proposed. A tax imposed by a country taking only a portion of the supply of a vintage wine would be met in part by a diversion of a larger portion of the supply to other markets, causing a rise of price in the short supply of the taxing country; if, however, the rarity of the wine were a considerable factor in its desirability, the rise of price might not appreciably check the demand, and so a slight shortage in our supply (accompanied by a slight increase of supply at lower price in other markets) might be attended by a rise of price which would compensate the producers for the tax.

Thus we see that, though an import duty tends to

fall in part on the producers where the latter are in a position to hold prices at a scarcity point, we cannot assure ourselves what proportion of the whole tax will lie upon him.

§4. It is important to approach the question of the incidence of import duties with a clear apprehension of the effects of taxes on " monopolised " or " scarcity" goods, because many economists, who support the policy of free imports, have assumed too absolutely the liability of the producers of these classes of imports to bear the entire tax. Though it is possible, in theory, at least, for a state to devise taxes on domestic monopolies or scarcity products which shall divert to the treasury the whole of the scarcity value, it is not even in theory possible to do this by such methods of taxation as are open to a foreign government which cannot deal directly with incomes, but only with produce entering a country.

In dealing with import duties on articles produced under conditions of monopoly or scarcity, we have seen that the possibility of making the producers bear the tax seemed to depend upon the fact that the price of the goods imported was not a competitive price, but one containing a surplus over and above the necessary expenses of production. If it is difficult, or impossible, under such circumstances to devise import duties which are certain to fall entirely on the producer, it is not to be expected that this can be done in the case of goods produced under ordinary competitive conditions.

Where agricultural or manufactured goods are produced by farmers or manufacturers whose competition keeps profits down towards a minimum, it would seem that no fund existed upon which an import duty could lie, and that any attempt to tax such imported articles must obviously defeat its end by checking production and raising prices.

§ 5. Now, while this rough analysis will be found to be substantially correct, we are not entitled to jump to the conclusion that "the consumers must pay all the tax."

Though there are here no scarcity rents at the margin upon which a duty may lie, there may be certain differential rents which can in part be made to bear a duty on imports.

Let us first take the case of agricultural produce entering a foreign market, not in competition with the home produce, but as the sole supply of some sort of food or raw material. Suppose that Great Britain could grow no wheat, but drew her entire supply from foreign lands. What would be the effect of placing a duty on this class of imports? It is clear that the duty could not be shifted by the importer who first paid it entirely on to the producer, because the farmers who grew wheat under conditions which made it only just worth while growing it would stop growing wheat, and the shortage of supply thus caused would raise the price; neither could it be shifted entirely on to the consumer in enhanced price, because the whole of the wheat supply could not be regarded as so absolutely "necessary" for consumption that raised prices would have no influence in reducing demand; and any reduction in demand would prevent the price rising to the full extent of the duty.

It is quite evident that some reduction in the supply of wheat will take place (the margin of cultivation rising) in consequence of the net price paid to the producers being lower than before, and that some reduction in the demand for wheat will take place in consequence of the net price charged to customers being higher. In other words, the duty will be divided in its incidence between producer and consumer.

In the case of an article of such prime importance in the standard of consumption as wheat, the elasticity of demand will be slight, or, in other words, a rise in the price to the consumer will have a comparatively slight effect upon demand. If, on the other hand, a considerable portion of the supply is produced under conditions of minimum profit to capital and labour, *i.e.* on land near the "margin," we have a combination of conditions which will force the consumer to pay most of the duty. If, at the same time that a duty is put on wheat, duties are also put on alternative goods, the elasticity of demand for wheat will be kept at its lowest, and the proportion of the tax which the consumer would bear will be at its largest. Of course, if alternative grains and other foods which were in some degree substitutes for wheat were left untaxed, the attempt of wheat growers to recoup themselves for the payment of the duty by raising prices might be largely defeated by the rapid shrinkage of demand. So, again, if very little wheat was grown near the margin of profit —most of it earning a high differential rent—a fall of net price might not drive out of cultivation a large quantity of wheat land. In either of these cases the producer might bear a considerable part of the duty.

Alternative uses of wheat land for other markets or for other agricultural uses, alternative foods on the part of the consumers, will play a large part in determining the incidence of the duty.

Since every fall of price must have some effect in checking supply, and every rise of price in checking demand, it is not possible that the entire burden of the tax should fall either on producer or consumer ; it must be shared.

What applies to agricultural produce will likewise apply to mining produce. An import duty will be divided in its incidence according to the restrictive elasticity of the supply and the demand, taking into consideration in each case the law of substitution. In as far as the duty falling on the mineowner renders it no longer profitable to work the poorer seams, it restricts the supply of ores; this restriction of supply raises the price of ore, until this rise of price, checking demand, brings about a new equilibrium of supply and demand at a price higher than the old price, but not higher by the full extent of the tax. Thus the duty here, too, is divided between producer and consumer.

§ 6. The case of an import duty on manufactured goods (not competing with home products) is different. The normal condition of the import trade is one of keen competition between manufacturers in the same or in different nations—a competition which tends to keep down profits to a common low level. Under these circumstances the producers cannot bear any considerable tax, and any duty which is paid by them must lead to a corresponding rise of price which shifts the burden on to the consumer. Nor does the rise of price necessarily stop there. For the first rise of price, as it checks demand for the manufactured imports, will tend to throw the manufacturers upon a restricted output, which is less economical than the larger output they formerly enjoyed; expenses of production per unit of the manufactured product will rise, and this rise will force a further rise of price.

This must, I think, be regarded as the normal result of a duty upon manufactured imports under ordinary conditions of well-established competition. Of course, there are circumstances which qualify this norm. Some businesses competing in the export trade may be far better equipped, more economically handled, and more advantageously placed than their competitors, and in consequence may be earning higher profits.

In so far as this is true, the effects of a duty upon the imported goods will approximate to the effects of a duty on agricultural produce ; the rise of price may not cover the entire duty, the poorer competitors will go under, unable to produce for the market, and the abnormal profits of the favourably situated manufacturers may be cut down by the duty. In a word, if in a manufacture there are differential profits which correspond to the differential rents of more fertile or better situated lands, a duty levied on the produce may fall on the former as we saw it fall upon the latter. There is, however, one not unimportant qualification to this power to put taxes on the foreign manufacturer. As its first effect is to crush weaker competitors, it will operate to promote combination among the smaller residue of strong competitors, who will be driven by a keen stimulus of self-defence to organise price-lists or combinations and maintain them.

Of course, it comes to this, that a duty upon manufactured imports can only be put upon producers in as far as competition has not already reduced their prices to a minimum profit, and weeding out the weaker competitors, left a number of equals. Where foreign countries send manufactured goods into another well-developed industrial country, it will seldom happen that the profits of such import trade can bear any considerable tax, unless the importer be a trust or "combine," a case with which we have already dealt.

The countries which could place a duty upon manufactured imports that might largely lie on producers are savage or backward countries, especially in the early days of their exploitation by more advanced industrial nations, whose traders often exchange cheap textile, metal, and other goods upon terms which are very profitable. A tax on beads, rum, and calico, by a fiscal statesman of Fiji or West Africa, when first brought into contact with civilised trading nations, would lie largely on producers. A nation such as Great Britain sending out exports in the shape of highly manufactured articles, shipping and financial services, largely restricted in the terms of their competition, and receiving in return from many sources foods, raw materials, and partly manufactured or wholly manufactured goods which represent surplus products, is probably getting a much larger aggregate of wealth, as measured by costs, than she pays in return. It is improbable that she could find many imports upon which she could safely and profitably impose duties, whereas it is quite probable that coun-

tries which receive her imports may find many
articles that will bear a tax.[1]

[1] The interesting investigation by which Dr. Cannan shows that
Great Britain has in recent years been obtaining increased quantities
of imports for a given quantity of exports supports this suggestion.
"Since 1885 the price of imports measured in exports has fallen 11 per
cent. for the United Kingdom and only 4 per cent. for Germany, while
the fall since 1881 has been 19 per cent. and 11 per cent. respectively.
This is a marked difference in both periods in our favour. . . . So far
as these tests show, both countries are carrying on their foreign trade
at an increasing advantage, but the advantage on the part of the
United Kingdom is greater. Of course the advantage in this greater
fall of prices of the goods we import than of those we export is doubtless due in part to the cheapening of transport, which counts as a
'cost' in the former but not in the latter set of prices. But it is also
probably attributable in part to the larger quantities of 'rents,'
'surplus profits,' 'high salaries,' contained in the prices of the goods
and services we export, than in the prices of the goods we import."

CHAPTER VI

THE INCIDENCE OF PROTECTIVE AND PREFERENTIAL DUTIES

§ 1

IT is proposed to tax agricultural produce and manufactured goods entering Great Britain from foreign countries. Who will bear the tax? British merchants will in the first instance pay the duties at the port of entry. No one, however, suggests that their profits, kept down by keen competition, are such as will enable or oblige them to bear any appreciable part of this new expense. They must recover it, either from the foreign producer in the lower prices they pay him for the goods they import, or from the home consumer in the higher prices they make him pay, or they must recover part of it from each.

In any case, the real incidence of the tax will take the shape of a change of price—a fall in prices paid to foreigners, a rise in prices paid by consumers, or both. In trying to trace the effect of a tax on prices, one principle must be kept constantly in mind, viz. that the immediate cause of every rise or fall of prices is a shift in the quantity of supply in relation to demand ; a rise of price can only come from a reduced supply or an increased demand, a fall of price from an increased supply or a reduced demand. Now it can be clearly seen that there are very few cases where the producer or the consumer will bear the entire tax, plus the cost of collection, in a direct rise or fall of prices. The only case where the consumer would bear this full expense is where an import duty was imposed upon a necessary of life, none of which could be produced at home.

If in Great Britain we could raise no wheat, and a duty were placed upon external supplies from all sources, a duty of 2s., 5s., or 10s. per quarter would tend to raise the prices to an equivalent extent. Even this statement, however, is only true on the assumption that *all* our present consumption of wheat were strictly necessary, and that a rise in its price would cause neither a reduction in the consumption of food nor a substitution of some other food, capable of being produced at home, for wheat. On such an assumption, the price paid by the consumer must rise to the full extent of the duty for the following reason. The first act of the merchant who paid the duty would be to reduce his importation of wheat, for he could not afford to buy so much at current prices ; this reduction of demand for foreign wheat in relation to the same supply will tend to bring down the price of wheat paid to the producer. Now some of the wheat supply only just pays to produce for export, it is said to be grown in "the margin of cultivation"; if it cannot get the former price, it will cease to enter the market. The slightest fall of price has some effect in reducing the supply; there is land in America and elsewhere which even a 2s. duty will put out of wheat-growing, or, what amounts to the same thing, there is land which would have gone into wheat-growing, but is now prevented by a fall of prices. A larger duty of 5s. or 10s. would, of course, reduce the supply of wheat more largely and more rapidly, if it were allowed to remain a tax on the producer. But directly the duty has begun to check the supply of wheat, by making it unprofitable to cultivate some wheat land which was cultivated before, the price of wheat in Great Britain would rise. If there were no "elasticity" in the demand for wheat, *i.e.* if all the wheat supply were absolutely "necessary," the rise of price would not diminish the sale of wheat: all the foreign wheat land must be kept in its former use, and this can only occur, *ex hypothesi*, on condition that the foreign grower gets his former net price and profit. The attempt, therefore, to throw any of the duty on the foreign producer would fail; the British consumer must pay the entire duty *plus* cost of collection in higher wheat prices.

The conditions under which the consumer here pays the whole of the tax are seen to be two: first, the duty is levied on the entire supply of the commodity (there being no home production); secondly, there is no elasticity of demand, a rise of price causing no decline in the quantity purchased.

§ 2. Now precisely because these conditions are not present in the case of a preferential duty upon agricultural imports or a protective duty upon manufactured imports, the duty cannot fall in its entirety upon the home consumer.

Take first the preferential duty upon wheat. As soon as a 2s. duty began to reduce American and other foreign prices for wheat by checking demand, it would begin to check wheat-growing "at the margin," but as it did this wheat prices would begin to rise from, say, the former level of 30s. to 32s. If they reached 32s. the foreign wheat supply for export would remain as before. But the price will not reach 32s. For under the preferential tariff any rise of price over the current 30s. must be supposed to stimulate the cultivation of wheat in Canada, and also to put back into wheat some British land. Though a 2s. duty may seem to some to "make no difference," it cannot seriously be doubted that it would turn the balance in some cases, and exercise a proportionate effect in stimulating Canadian cultivation and in preventing some wheat land in Great Britain from going out of cultivation. The notion that a duty, because it is small, may have no effect, is, of course, unthinkable; its effect will only be slighter and slower than the effect of a 5s. or 10s., into which it will tend to grow.

If, therefore, there is *any* colonial or British land which can be rendered profitable for wheat-growing or other agricultural use by a rise of price less than is represented by the duty, to that extent the price to consumers will be prevented from rising to the full extent of the duty. The price must rise, for otherwise there is no inducement to the colonial or home grower to produce more wheat than he produces now; it cannot rise to the full extent of the tax, unless we suppose such rise of price to have no effect whatever in stimulating the increase of that part of the supply which enjoys the rise of price without feeling the tax.

The notion, often broached, that the price of our wheat supply is fixed at Chicago by the price set on American export wheat, and that, since Americans would have to recoup themselves for the British duty by a proportionate rise of their prices, the Canadian and even the home producer would reap the benefit of this rise, though in a measure true as regards immediate price changes, has no validity in the long run. Prices of wheat depend in the long run, not on Chicago or other speculators, but upon the conditions of growing wheat on the worst-placed or the poorest land engaged in or available for growing it. If by a preferential tariff we can substitute somewhat worse or less accessible land in Canada or Great

Britain for better land in the United States or Argentina, we shall undoubtedly have to pay a higher price for our wheat, but that price need not, and indeed cannot be, higher by the full extent of the preferential duty.

So the incidence of such a duty would come to be divided between the British consumer and the foreign producer. Some foreign producers would simply cease to produce for our market, others would continue to produce, bearing some part of the duty in the lower prices they got from importing merchants. It is not possible accurately to conjecture what proportion of the duty would fall on producers, what on consumers, without knowing the precise agricultural and industrial resources of all the countries contributing to our supply, so as to be able to calculate the effect of a given rise of wheat prices in driving out of wheat cultivation foreign lands which contribute to our supply, and in stimulating the cultivation of colonial lands. As regards the latter, it is a question, not merely of quantity and quality of land, but of railroad and general industrial enterprise, and of the rate and character of settlement upon new lands. Considering how large a proportion of our wheat and other agricultural supplies we derive from foreign, as compared with colonial and home sources, and the heavy initial outlay in substituting unbroken land in the Canadian North-West for the American fields which now so largely supply us, it is probable that the price of wheat, at any rate for many years to come, would rise nearly to the limit set by a preferential duty.

§ 3. But the full burden which such a duty would impose upon the British consumer is, of course, not adequately represented in this first result. The prime evil of a protective duty is that it tends to take more from the consumer in enhanced prices than it procures for the treasury. For the higher price is paid upon the part of the supply which does not pay the tax, as well as upon that part which does. If, for example, the result of a 2s. preferential duty on grain were to raise the price 1s. 6d. per quarter, while the treasury would only receive £3,300,000, the tax upon the quantity imported in 1902 (amounting to 176,000,000 cwts.), the British consumers would have to pay £6,957,000 in enhanced prices upon the total foreign, colonial, and home supply, amounting to 371,000,000 cwts. Thus the sum paid by the British consumers as a result of the duty would amount to more than twice the sum raised by the treasury through a duty, one quarter of which was paid by the producer, three quarters by the consumer.

§ 4. In the case of a protective duty of 10 per cent. on manufactured goods the same line of reasoning is generally applicable, though the extent to which the tax can be shifted on to the foreign producer will differ more widely in the several classes of commodities. In the ordinary case, where foreign manu-

G

facturers, in competition with one another as well as with our manufacturers, are selling goods in our market, the effect of any protective duty must be to check their sales, for those who are working so near the margin of profit that they can only just undersell our manufacturers at current prices will not be able to meet the demand of the importer that they shall lower their prices to recoup him for the payment of the import duty. The supply of goods being thus reduced by the stoppage of weaker import goods, while demand stands as before, prices must rise. They cannot rise to the full extent of the 10 per cent. duty except on two improbable suppositions : first, that a rise of price will have no effect in checking demand ; secondly, that none of the foreign goods can afford to pay any of the tax, so that, until the price rises the full 10 per cent., all imports are kept out.

Even in the latter case, which is that of a prohibitive duty, it does not follow that the price to the consumer, as the result of substituting home for foreign goods, must rise to the full extent of the duty. Whether it will do so depends on two conditions of home production and home competition. If the article excluded be a necessary or prime convenience, the demand for which is not materially affected by a moderate rise of price, while the home supply cannot be enlarged to displace the former foreign supply save by employing inferior appliances or labour, the price might rise nearly to the full amount of the duty plus expenses of collection. In no other case could this happen. If the article excluded were a luxury, any considerable rise of price, due to the cessation (or even a large reduction) of import, would commonly be attended by a considerable fall-off in demand, and a new price-level not much above the old might be reached by a slight stimulation of home production. If the home product were only slightly undersold by the foreign goods, upon which the duty is now laid, it appears that the substitution might be effected without any considerable rise of prices to consumers, or any large reduction in the total supply. The extent of the rise of price and the relative incidence of the tax depend upon elasticity of demand and of supply, i.e. how far a given rise of price will check demand of consumers and stimulate supply of producers at home, and how far a given fall of price will check supply abroad and stimulate demand of consumers there. The question is one of delicate readjustment on both sides. A general protective duty of 10 per cent. on foreign manufactures must have a variety of different effects on different classes of goods.

The only conclusions of general validity are those which hold of all protective or preferential duties.

First. They must raise prices to the consumer.

Second. They cannot raise prices to the full extent of the duty.

Third. Since the higher prices will be paid, not only on the imported goods, but on the entire home supply as well, the sum paid by the consuming public will commonly exceed the sum received by the treasury. Where a "protective" duty thoroughly protects, excluding foreign goods for the benefit of home producers, the treasury receives nothing and the consumer pays a price which approximates to the old price plus the duty.

§ 5. This argument, so far as relates to home prices, is based upon the supposition that genuinely free competition is maintained among British producers. The conclusion that the rise of prices due to protection will not normally cover the whole duty, so as to throw the entire burden on the consumer, presupposes that no agreement takes place among British producers as to prices. But in actual practice it is likely to be otherwise. Even under free imports British manufacturers are constantly engaged in limiting their competition by fixing price-lists to which they more or less adhere. Protection greatly stimulates this process. Under a protective tariff British producers would have a greater inducement to combine upon a rise of prices, and such combination would be more feasible. In highly developed industries a protective tariff favours combination, and its necessary effect is to raise prices to the limit set by the duty.   Thus, where under strictly competitive conditions the consumer would not bear the whole burden of the tax in higher prices, the normal tendency of actual trade is to compel him to do so.

§ 6.   One point of critical importance remains.   In the foregoing argument I have confined myself to tracing the effect of separate duties upon special markets. But where a system of protective duties is adopted, the effects are not single, but cumulative.   If a 2*s.* duty were imposed on wheat or a 10 per cent. duty upon a particular manufacturing import, we saw that the natural result would be a rise of price to something less than the amount of the duty.   But when a general protective tariff is adopted, prices tend to rise to the limit of any tax.   Our supposition that wheat prices might rise 1*s.* 6*d.* was based on an assumption that wages and other expenses of production of British farmers remained as before the adoption of the new fiscal policy.   But if the price, not only of food, but of all manufactured goods for labourer and for employer, is going to rise by the operation of an all-round tariff, the normal expenses of raising wheat at home will rise, and this increase will force prices of wheat up beyond the 1*s.* 6*d.*, by making it unprofitable to grow wheat on some land where otherwise it could have been grown.   So the effect of the general tariff will be to make wheat prices approximate the 2*s.* limit, and when they do this the farmers will quite naturally complain that the

" protection " afforded them is inadequate, because as much foreign wheat enters as before, and though their money price for wheat is higher, their raised expenses of production makes farming no more profitable than under free imports. This is the force which in France and Germany has been effective in inducing a series of increases of the duty upon agricultural goods.

The same argument applies to the manufacturing tariff. The separate effect of a 10 per cent. tariff on a class of goods may be to substitute British for foreign goods by a rise of 6 or 8 per cent. in price. But that effect presupposes expenses of production based on the same prices of food and other commodities as before. But agricultural protection will have raised the expenses of the food of town-workers, the 10 per cent. duty on other classes of manufactured or semi-manufactured goods will raise the price of plant, machinery, and perhaps raw material; on every hand the manufacturer will find expenses of production higher than before. Thus he too will be impelled to a rise of the prices of his goods towards the full 10 per cent. which marks his limit of protection; he too will then clamour for a rise of the 10 to 20, 30, or 50 per cent.

The full burden of a protective tariff borne by the members of the protecting nation is measured by the diminished national production of wealth due to an artificial diversion of producing power from more productive to less productive employments. This waste of efficiency of capital and labour is everywhere represented in rising expenses of production, which tend to raise prices in all protected industries towards the limit set by existing duties, thus forcing them perpetually to demand increased protection.

CHAPTER VII

HOW THE BALANCE OF IMPORTS AND EXPORTS IS ACHIEVED

§ 1

WHILE it is generally recognised that in the processes of international trade a balance of import and export values is maintained if a sufficient period of time be taken, it is not always clearly understood how this balance is maintained. To say that imports cannot exceed exports because a nation, like an individual, must in the long run pay for what it buys is a true but an inadequate solution of the problem. It is precisely because a nation is not an individual that the simple answer is not sufficient. A, B, C, D, members of the British nation, trade with E, F, G, H, members of other nations; if A stops buying the goods he used to buy from E, thereby reducing the aggregate imports of his nation, how does A's action prevent F, G, H from buying some goods they used to buy from B, C, D, thereby reducing the aggregate exports of A's nation? The mere statement that exports must balance imports because people must pay for what they buy requires further explanation, because the persons who are the direct payees are not the same persons who have done the buying. If some British firms cease to buy from foreigners, other British firms will cease to sell to foreigners ; if some British firms increase their purchases abroad, other British firms must increase their sales abroad ; if some German or American firms "dump" increased quantities of goods upon our shores, other Germans or Americans must either buy more goods from us or cause other foreigners to buy more goods from us, so that the "dumping" induces an expansion of our export trade. These propositions, though quite true, do not at first sight seem involved in the statement that a nation must pay for what she buys.

A good deal of mystification has arisen by the nature of the concrete illustrations to which resort is had in arguing the matter. If I buy a motor-car for £500 in Paris instead of buying it in London, how shall I be compelling Frenchmen or some other foreigners to buy an equivalent amount of English goods? It will surely be better for English trade if I pay a little more for an English-made car. Now, this sort of illustrative argument, which seems so convincing to the tyro in economic reasoning, has a fatal defect. The illustration is on too small a scale. All changes of trade are brought about through changes of prices, and if too small an example be taken, a single act of purchase, it seems absurd to impute to it any influence upon the price in the trade, still less on general prices in a country. To show how the purchase of a single motor-car in Paris will alter the relation between British and Continental prices of commodities in general is impossible by reason of the triviality of the cause; or, taking the industrial instead of the financial side, it is equally impossible to show that so small an incident can affect the flow of capital and labour as between the motor-car industry and other industries, thus again altering general prices in England and on the Continent. No network of reasoning can be made so fine that a fictitious fish, made small enough, cannot get through. To argue the issue intelligibly, cases of sufficiently large dimensions must be taken.

§ 2. Let our problem be to prove how a stoppage of imports must cause a corresponding stoppage of exports. There are two modes of proof, the first financial, the second concretely industrial. Let us suppose that a prohibitive tariff were to stop entirely the imports of dairy produce into Great Britain from Denmark and other Continental countries for which we pay some £30,000,000 per annum. English importers of dairy produce no longer draw bills to this amount and send them abroad in payment. Foreign merchants who are buying goods of various sorts from England are in the habit of paying for these goods, not by sending cash, but by buying from foreign bankers and brokers bills on London. Since the number of these bills is now reduced to the extent of £30,000,000 per annum, the supply of them will be short in relation to the demand, and the price paid on the Continent for the use of this convenient mode of payment will be raised. A merchant wishing to buy from England must now pay a larger number of francs and centimes in order to make a payment of £100 to England. That is equivalent to a rise of prices of English goods to Continental buyers, and must operate in some measure to check purchases and so to stop English exports. In England, on the other hand, there will be a corresponding superfluity of bills on Paris, Berlin, etc., the price of these bills will sink, an English sovereign will buy a larger number of francs and centimes. This means a fall of Continental prices for English buyers, and will stimulate English merchants and importers to buy more foreign goods in place of the dairy produce we have ceased to buy, and to restore the old aggregate of imports.

We have here a double process of automatic adjustment, a shrinkage of English exports and an expansion of foreign imports, tending to produce a new balance of international trade.

But let us suppose that this first mode of readjustment is incomplete, and that there still remains on the Continent a deficiency of bills on London as compared with other bills in the clearance system. What occurs next is a reversion to the gold basis of payment to meet the deficit. Gold begins to flow into England and swells the reserve of the Bank of England. Under ordinary circumstances this increase of gold will cause the Bank to lower its rate of discount, and money on loan will be cheap.

This cheapness of money for advances will cause increased borrowing. People who want money want it for one purpose, viz. to buy with it goods and services they could not otherwise buy. The result of cheap money will therefore be an increase in the rate of demand for goods and services, in relation to the rate of supply,[1] thus causing a general rise of prices. This general rise of prices will check the export trade, foreigners preferring to buy more cheaply elsewhere. Each step in this process is, of course, reversed upon the Continent. The flow of gold to England will raise rates of discount abroad, make money dear for borrowers, check borrowing, reduce demand in relation to supply, lower general prices, make it more profitable for English merchants to buy abroad, and so increase the imports side of the balance. Thus

---

[1] It is, of course, to be borne in mind that borrowers who have thus increased facilities of obtaining money are generally business firms which seek to purchase more capital and to employ more labour for production, thus enhancing the supply of all sorts of commodities. This secondary effect, an increase of the rate of supply, serves as an automatic check upon the continuous tendency of "cheap money" to raise prices.

we see how the stoppage of £30,000,000 of dairy imports into England has set in operation financial forces which, partly by substituting increased quantities of other imports for the prohibited dairy produce, partly by checking English exports, redress the balance between the aggregate of English imports and exports.

§ 3. Turning from financial to concretely industrial movements, we can see the same process of readjustment. The cessation of trade in dairy produce with England, damaging the dairy industry of Denmark, Holland, etc., will divert into other industrial channels the industrial energy, the capital and labour which would otherwise have gone into the upkeep and further development of the dairy trade. Making all due allowance for waste in the transfer of capital and labour already specialised, and for the substitution of industries "naturally" less productive for the more productive dairy industry, this diversion of a larger quantity of capital and labour into other Danish and Dutch industries will, by increasing the rate of supply of these commodities in relation to demand, lower prices. This fall of prices will have its due effect in stimulating English purchases of foreign goods to displace the former purchase of dairy produce. If we look at the effects in England we shall find the converse series of changes. The stoppage of dairy imports, by raising prices in England for all dairy produce, will bring large quantities of capital and labour into this branch of agricultural industry. We are not entitled to assume that a large mass of capital and labour remains permanently idle waiting for such opportunities. The greater application of industrial energy to dairy work will mean a smaller application in all other industrial employments : thus the rate of supply in other industries shrinks in relation to demand, and so there is a general rise of prices. This general rise of English prices, however small, will have its due effect in checking the purchases of English goods by foreigners, whose general prices, as we see, are falling. So English exports are reduced to balance the reduction of imports by stopping the entrance of Danish and Dutch dairy produce. Incidentally it may be remarked that the new balance brought about by automatic readjustments to compensate an artificial disturbance of the kind supposed will be a balance less advantageous in terms of real wealth to both parties. The capital and labour violently displaced from the dairy industry in Denmark and Holland will be *ex hypothesi* less productively employed in the other industries to which it has recourse, thus diminishing the aggregate of real wealth produced in these countries, and reacting injuriously also upon Great Britain in obliging her to take a smaller quantity of real wealth than before in the processes of international exchange which she still continues to employ.

Similarly, in England, the same artificial intervention has drawn a large amount of industrial energy to leave other employments in which it would have produced a larger quantity of real wealth in order to produce a smaller quantity of dairy wealth to which a tariff has imputed a fictitious value. The aggregate production of wealth in England is reduced by this artificial diversion, and some of this injury passes to Continental nations in the processes of international exchange.

CHAPTER VIII

WHAT A NATION BUYS AND WHAT IT PAYS WITH

IT has been shown that the principles of exchange of commodities are essentially the same, whether the exchange takes place between members of the same nation and is called internal trade, or between members of different nations and is called international trade. The tendency for commodities to exchange in accordance with the ratio of their marginal cost of production is not, under Free Trade, impeded more in the latter case than in the former by the lack of complete mobility of capital and labour. Wherever fairly large, constant, and various trade relations exist between different nations, a keen comparison is made of the efficiency of capital and labour in the two countries with reference to their natural resources, and on this basis is established an international division of labour which is at once the result and the cause of international trade. Just in proportion as that com-

parison of international efficiency is fully and fairly
maintained is this division of labour effective in
securing the maximum of world-wealth and in
enabling the members of each co-operant nation
to secure a larger quantity of wealth for themselves
than they otherwise could obtain. Efficiency in
division of labour leads each nation to produce
more, efficiency in exchange enables it to consume
more; and as these two efficiencies are interdepen-
dent, the doctrine of the utility of free exchange
may equally be regarded as a producer's or a
consumer's policy. The complete economy demands, as we have seen, perfect mobility of
capital and labour or the abolition of non-competing
groups. But the fact that this condition is not
reached, and that, therefore, commodities cannot
exchange in the exact ratio of their marginal costs,
does not one whit impair the advantage of maintaining a policy of free exchange among commodities actually produced under these unequal
conditions. Free exchange always *tends* to equalise
the costs of production and so to enforce a better
division of labour.

Nations whose members trade freely with one
another will therefore establish a division of labour
on a basis of relative efficiency for the various processes of production. Each nation will produce for
itself the greater part of the commodities and
services it requires, though these commodities and

services may be of the same sort for each nation ; the production of bulky and of perishable goods, of special goods adapted to the national or local taste, the final processes of production in many trades where the demands of a fluctuating market must be met, the entire vast trades of internal transport, building, and of distribution, almost all the professional and other intellectual work, domestic and other personal services, these departments, constituting the greater part of the national industry, are by their nature precluded from international division of labour.

Though increased speed and cheapness of transport, and improved methods of preserving perishables, throw an increasing number of commodities into the arena of the international market, the proportion of the national productive energy submitted to international division of labour at any given time is subject to tolerably rigid limitations, and, as we have seen, there is reason to believe that the proportion of that energy will diminish in nations which attain the higher reaches of civilisation, demanding more highly individualised forms of national consumption and devoting a larger share of their effective demand to non-material goods.

§ 2. The extractive arts of agriculture and mining, manufactures, and the services of sea-transport and finance form the staples of division of labour among nations. Every nation does some of each of these kinds of work for itself, but it does very little of some kinds, a great deal of other kinds, using the surplus of the latter to purchase enough of the former to meet its requirements for consumption.

There can be no fixity in this division of international labour; under Free Trade or under Protection, what any nation buys from other nations, and what it pays with, will be changing all the time. In proportion as free exchange prevails, each nation will specialise along the lines of the relative advantages it enjoys at the time for the various industries. Where strongly marked, persistent natural conditions of climate, soil, position, are bases of an important national industry, that industry will have a high degree of permanence as a factor in the make-up of the export trade. The strong, lasting export trades of Great Britain—cotton, coal, shipping, banking—all enjoy some such element of natural superiority as a basis of other acquired aptitudes.

The adoption of protective systems by a number of other nations, in order to counteract such natural or acquired aptitudes, may, of course, succeed in preventing a nation from using to the full this natural choice of purchasing power in the shape of exports to pay for the imports she requires. But for the protective tariffs of the large Continental countries and of the United States, Great Britain would probably be somewhat more specialised in textile, metal, and certain other manufactures than she is now, sending out larger quantities of these sorts of goods to buy her imports with. Probably the total volume of her export and import trade would be larger than it is. But the embargo placed by foreign protective systems on these British goods by no means represents a corresponding diminution—(a) of British exports in general, (b) of these classes of exports in particular. For there will be two readjustments in British export trade, as the result of a tariff placed by certain foreign nations upon certain classes of imports from Great Britain. We shall in the first place divert our export trade in these excluded goods from highly protected to lowly protected or open markets of other countries, *ex hypothesi* a less profitable trade, and probably for this very reason a somewhat smaller trade. In the second place, we shall send out other exports to the high-protective countries to take the place of the excluded exports, if we can find any goods where our relative advantage of production is nearly as great as in the case of the former exports, and where no considerable import duty keeps us out. Just as each nation finds out, under conditions of free exchange, the kinds of goods and the quantity of each it pays her to produce and exchange for various quantities of other kinds of goods she cannot make or make cheaply, so now the artificial rearrangement of industries in foreign countries arising from a tariff will compel a free-trade country to change the current, the volume, and to some extent the nature of her export trade. She will buy her imports partly from different nations than before, partly from the same nations, but indirectly. Nor will she import the same proportions of the same goods as before. For the difference in her modes, sizes, and places of payment will change the kinds and amounts of goods she will find it most profitable to import.

The following is a practical illustration of the application of this theory in modern commerce :—

"Take the trade between the United States and this country. We import thence in value about four times as much as we export thither. Part of this excess comes in discharge of debt of one kind or another ; but much of it is paid for indirectly by exports of our manufactures to countries from which the United States receive large supplies of tropical and other produce, but to which they send comparatively little merchandise of any kind in return. Among these countries are India, China, Brazil, Cuba, the British West Indies, Colombia, Ecuador, Venezuela, Japan, and Egypt. To all of these the exports of British productions are in excess—often very largely—of our imports from them. It is clear, therefore, that although we export very much less merchandise to the United States from the United Kingdom than they send to us, or, to put the matter in another way, the United States by their high tariff prevent us from paying them directly for the enormous amount of produce which we take from them, they do not and cannot prevent us from supplying our manufactures in payment for the produce which they draw from tropical and other regions. Why? Simply because our manufactures, suited to the wants of those regions, are cheaper, i.e. produced at less cost than their own."

It is quite evident that the protective policy of several great nations, restricting their export trade with one another as compared with the trade each continues to do with the richest of the free-import countries, viz. Great Britain, has been largely instrumental in forcing freight-service and banking to the fore among our modes of payment for our imports. It is equally evident that the point of great insistence by Tariff Reformers, viz. that our recent trade with protected countries shows a slower growth than with non-protected countries, so far as it is correct, merely signifies this process of adaptation on the part of British trade seeking the lines of least resistance or greatest receptiveness for the movement of our exports.

§ 3. What we buy and what we pay with must be in a continual state of flux, under free exchange or under protection, unless the latter system leads to complete industrial isolation accompanied by stagnation in population and the arts alike of production and consumption.

The character and proportions of the foreign trade of a progressive nation must always be changing, and the more large, various, and profitable that trade is, the more numerous and important will be the changes. If then we examine the export trades of any country, we shall expect to find some of them dwindling and others growing. A dwindling export trade may, of course, signify the successful competition of foreigners in their own markets or in neutral markets which we once held.

But it may mean something quite different, viz. either the increase of domestic consumption, which has at once raised the value of these goods and left no surplus for export, or that other trades have grown up with which we find we can more economically make our export payments. Both of these causes of the apparent decay of an export trade are *primâ facie* indications of increased national wealth. In the case of the recent decline of the woollen and worsted export trade, both causes are doubtless operative. The largely increased consumption of wool in the manufacture indicates that a growth of domestic trade has checked the export trade; one reason for the decline of woollen exports is that our own people are becoming better clad. The other reason is that the woollen is our oldest manufacture, the greater improvements in mechanical inventions and in the development of markets therefore coming earlier it has reached a stage in which further reductions in cost of production are relatively slight; other newer industries have sprung up in which for a time our relative superiority of production as compared with other nations is greater than in the case of wool. It is at present more profitable for us to buy an increasing proportion of our imports with coal, machinery, and ships than with woollen and linen goods. The chief reason for the positive or relative decline of most export trades which are the subjects of commiseration is, not the protective tariffs of foreign countries, but the competition of other British industries which have secured a larger proportion of our export trade for themselves. For though neither our export nor our import trade can rightly be regarded as a fixed inexpansive quantity, so that a new cheap British manufacture can only force a foreign market by displacing some other British export, our examination of the financial mechanism of international trade has made it evident that a selection of different kinds of import and export goods is continually being made by merchants in accordance with the rise and fall of prices for various kinds of goods in their own as compared with the several foreign countries. The practical problem which is being worked out at any given moment by the financial and commercial class in various foreign countries who call out British exports is how best to balance in terms of British exports the amount of British import values represented by bills of exchange in their hands. We saw that any increase or decrease of these bills in London must act on foreign and British prices so as to stimulate or depress British exports, and so to maintain a balance of import and export trade. As some British prices will fall or rise more than others, the foreigners who call out British exports will fasten more on those where the relative fall of price is greater, or the relative rise of prices less. In this way foreign buyers are continually selecting some kinds of goods for our export trade, rejecting others.

The trades in which we are making more rapid progress as compared with foreign countries will naturally be favoured in this selection of exports from Great Britain. Behind this foreign selection, the competition of British trades among themselves may be said to determine the place they shall severally occupy in our export trade. At one time textiles, cotton, woollen, silk, linen in various changing proportions, form the greater part of our export values ; then, partly in substitution, partly as a result of expansion, the metal trades take a more prominent place ; later still, special metal trades connected with machinery forge ahead and vie with the closely related industry of shipbuilding and with coal to make the pace.

Taking our import trade as a given quantity, we thus see that the make-up of the return cargo of exports will be constantly shifting, as a result, partly of changes in foreign demand, partly of changes in the internal conditions of British industries as compared with one another and with the corresponding foreign industries. It will pay us better to send, and it will pay them better to receive, a different sort of cargo this year than we sent last year to represent each £1,000,000 of exports.

§ 4. But, of course, our import trade is not really a

fixed quantity. Just as an increased demand for foreign goods on our part compels foreigners to find British goods which they will buy in return (unless they can get British industries to use the goods they send as capital and to pay them interest alone), so an increased demand for British exports may issue from foreigners, who will thus oblige us to receive more imports (unless we in our turn prefer to increase our foreign investments). Imports and exports are, as we have seen, mutual determinants, so far as quantities of values are concerned : an increase or shrinkage of the one compels a corresponding increase or shrinkage of the other. If, then, even a fixed volume of export trade will be continually liable to changes of its make-up, a constant change of volume will impress an even greater fluctuation on the export trades.

§ 5. The mystery made of investments as a factor in the balance contains nothing essentially mysterious. There is nothing in the financial mechanism for securing a balance of imports and exports to insist that either side shall pay immediately in full for everything it receives. A foreign government or a group of members of a foreign nation may borrow from a group of Englishmen without setting in operation any financial movement requiring foreigners immediately to restore a corresponding amount of wealth to England. A loan from England to a foreign government or a group of foreigners is an order for British goods to be delivered without payment; when the foreigner receives this order he translates it into a demand for goods, steel rails, engines, machinery, etc.; but instead of putting into the money market bills of exchange, which would, as we have seen, force a present or early payment in goods, he returns to the lenders scrip entitling them to receive a small percentage of the value of the goods they sent out, in goods representing yearly interest, the equivalent repayment of the loan being indefinitely delayed. Every such loan when it takes place represents a quantity of exports for which no corresponding imports are required in the ordinary balance of trade; the only paper put on the money market compelling imports is the certificates of interest or dividend, which force imports in the same way as bills of exchange. While loans are being thus effected the creditor nation is sending out exports which exceed her imports by the amount of the loans, less the interest from the sums previously loaned. When a nation, as is the case with Great Britain, has effected enormous loans during a long series of years, the imports which represent the annual interest on these loans may largely exceed the new capital invested abroad in any single year, especially if, as is likely, a substantial part of her increase of foreign investments takes the form of refraining from demanding the interest on former investments and allowing it to accumulate as fresh loan.

The practical bearing of the changes in the tide of investment upon the volume of imports and exports, and the annual balance of the same, is brought home by the analysis of recent British investments presented by Mr. Schuster in a paper read at the Institute of Bankers,[1] in which the writer points out that the flow of British capital into foreign investments during the seventies and eighties received a notable check from the financial troubles of South America in 1891, followed in 1893 by the Australian banking crisis, and in subsequent years by the currency disturbances in the United States.

"In 1896 new capital applied for again rose to 153 millions. The demand was not so much for foreign or colonial securities, but mainly for home investments and industrial undertakings of all sorts. The company promoter was hard at work, and in many cases not for the benefit of the community at large or of the industries which he took in hand. We have thus a distinct change in the channels of investment; we deliberately turned away from foreign and colonial enterprises in favour of investments in the home markets, and to that may be directly due part of the lack of expansion in our exports, which would have followed naturally had we placed the capital abroad, and also the increase in our imports for the home industries, which receive much of their material from abroad."

[1] December 16, 1903.

Finally, the effects of the South African War must be taken into account.

" But the end of 1899 is the date of the outbreak of the South African War, and that war must naturally have had such a disturbing effect on the whole of our trade that no conclusion can possibly be drawn from the variations taking place since that period. It is evident that the purchases of war material of all sorts must have swelled our imports to a very large degree, that Government purchases abroad of foodstuffs, animals, and a variety of articles which were shipped direct to South Africa without appearing in our trade returns must have naturally turned all the exchanges against us, and that all this vast expenditure resulted in keeping the value of money at a higher level here than in other centres. Until the outbreak of the war, there is nothing in the indications of the exchanges to warrant the assumption that our commercial condition had resulted in affecting our position as the cheapest money market, which is so essential for the maintenance of our supremacy as the bankers of the world. But I think the above-mentioned facts show that special and exceptional reasons closed our most important markets, or at least greatly impeded our exports to them. We declined to lend money to foreign countries, and thus prevented their purchases from us ; by far the greatest part of our savings were invested at home, mostly in loans to local authorities, and that in itself led to a very important increase in our imports ; it stimulated the building trade, the development of electrical works and undertakings, and a great deal of the material had to be imported, if only for the reason that our factories at home were not in a position to supply the demand."

Thus it appears that no inconsiderable part of the widening gap between import and export values will be due to the fact that foreign and colonial investments have taken of late a smaller share of our spare capital than formerly, the increased volume of interest from foreign investments proceeding from a ripening into profit of earlier investments.

But whilst this loaning, payment of interest, and repayment of capital may be treated independently of the current interchange of commodities between nations in an investigation of the nature of the balance of import and export trade, the fact that each of these proceedings involves a supply and a demand for actual commodities causes price changes in the loaning and borrowing countries which have subtle and sometimes important reactions on the volume and character of the entire current of normal trade. To take the rudest of examples: a foreign loan negotiated in London, which involved large orders for British ships, or steam engines for early delivery, would obviously, by raising prices in these and their related trades, affect the availability of these kinds of goods for ordinary export trade, i.e. we should pay for our imports less in these kinds, more in other kinds of goods. By raising somewhat the general level of British prices, moreover, such large loans on special exports would reduce somewhat the volume of ordinary export and therefore of import trade. If it involved, again, not an increase of the aggregate of our national saving, but a diversion of capital from British to foreign investments, other forces affecting prices and volume of foreign trade would be set in operation.

Thus the amount and character of borrowing, payment of interest, and repayment of loans which are blended with the normal interchange of commodities between nations will have delicate reactions in the make-up of the export and import cargoes, as well as upon the volume. There is no subtler question in international economics than that of the determination of the flow and distribution of capital; and the rapid growth of mobility of capital, which we have elsewhere discussed, is destined to play an increasing part in the operations of international exchange.

The magnitude and the nature of this flow of capital from nation to nation are not, however, such as to invalidate the general principles of the balance of imports and exports in international trade ; they complicate the current accounts, but do not vitally affect the business policy.

§ 6. It must, of course, be kept in mind that though in one sense there is no fixity in volume and make-up of foreign trade, there is fixity in another sense. Taking the industry of the world as it exists at any given time, there is an absolutely right volume and make-up of the import and the export trade of each country, the quantity which each, if it understood all the actual facts of world industry, would secure. In fact, the whole intelligence of the mercantile and financial classes which operate foreign commerce is constantly engaged in seeking to achieve and maintain this economically right balance of trade between the several nations. What quantities of what kinds of goods each nation buys, and what quantities of what kinds of goods it pays with, are directly determined by the delicate mechanism of international finance, which, registering the productive capacities of the several nations in the various industries, directs the flow of free capital and labour into the most productive channels, and so elicits those surpluses of various kinds of wealth, over and above the needs of home consumption, which form the substance of international commerce.

CHAPTER IX

CAN PROTECTIVE COUNTRIES "SUCK"
A FREE-TRADE COUNTRY?

§ 1

THE limits on mobility of capital and labour in most industries, and the defective intelligence of the business world at large, prevent the machinery of international finance from achieving more than a fraction of the full economy of division of labour and interchange of wealth which it is designed to secure. The chief harm of protective tariffs, bounties, or preferences consists in impeding further the operation of these beneficent forces aiming to secure for each nation the particular volume and make-up of import and export trade which is at once most profitable for her and for the commonwealth of nations. To the wastes occasioned by immobility and ignorance it adds a new artificial waste, setting nations to do work they cannot do so well as other nations, and thereby preventing them from doing better work. It makes a nation buy abroad a smaller quantity and different qualities of goods than it would be good for her to buy, and it makes her pay for them in larger quantities and different qualities of goods than is good for her to pay. To a less extent and in various degrees the tariff of each nation inflicts similar injuries on each other nation of the commercial world.

Although it will be manifest that the main injury of a protective system falls on the country that adopts it, and only a smaller injury upon another country thus restrained in commerce with her, it may be useful to examine the suggestion that a number of protective countries, each exercising this restraint, may inflict blows upon a free-trade country whose cumulative force will virtually destroy her trade and suck out her available capital. It has been suggested that Great Britain is or may be in such a case.

The danger commonly indicated assumes a twofold character. A ring of protective nations may, by putting up high tariff walls, exclude our goods from their shores, while at the same time their producers, enjoying the security of a protected and high-priced home market, "dump" their artificially cheapened goods upon our shores, underselling our producers, and taking their trade.

Now it is evident to anyone who grasps the first principle of foreign trade, viz. that it consists in exchange of commodities, that the two alleged dangers are mutually destructive. If protective nations are refusing to receive our goods, they cannot continue to dump their goods at any price upon our shores.

They must take payment either in current imports from us (directly or through intermediate nations), or in liens upon our capital which they are engaged in depreciating by the very process in question, and which would be absolutely valueless by the time they had carried their policy to its logical conclusion. If nations "dump" cheap goods on us and try to evade payment by putting up tariffs, this policy does not mean that they are not paid, but that they are paid in a smaller quantity of dearer British goods (or their foreign equivalents) instead of the larger quantity of cheaper goods they would have received in free exchange. What their joint protective and dumping policy does is to alter the division of employments in Great Britain, the make-up of our export trade, and the proportion of the exports which go to various foreign countries. What they dump is likely to be raw material for some of our trades, for most commodities, though they be finished manufactures or foodstuffs, are raw materials for some trades; these trades, directly subsidised by the foreigner, will send in their products over the tariff wall which the same foreigner sets up to counteract his own bounty on exports. A widespread system of "dumping" would also mean cheap commodities to British consumers, would help to keep money wages low and thus again would keep down expenses of production for British producers in all trades. When we remember that the exact converse of these forces are operating in the protective and dumping countries to raise the expenses of production in general, and particularly in trades where goods sold high at home in order to sell low abroad are raw materials, we perceive the mutually destructive nature of dumping and protection. Even if the protective tariff of each country were so arranged as to prevent us from sending exports into those countries from trades fed by the dumped articles, we should send them into neutral countries with which they also trade, and underselling them, as they themselves would have assisted us to do, we should force our payment on them through the indirect methods of roundabout trade. Seeing that the costs, alike of dumping and protection, fall in the main on expenses of production in the protective country, it is easy to understand how the bounty-fed industries in free-import Great Britain can force markets, either directly in these protective countries wherever the tariff wall is lower than usual, or in countries where tariffs are lower or non-existent.

§ 2. If we suppose that there are no other free import or low-tariff nations, and that the ring of protectionist nations is so infatuated as to put up protective tariffs on all our export trade, they have not only stopped our trade, but their own as well, even the dumping which is part of it; for no "tariff reformer" is likely to suggest that "dumping" can go on *in vacuo*, foreigners taking nothing in return. Moreover, the least reflection will make it manifest that long before our foreign trade was crushed by this protectionist ring, the trade between the protectionist countries themselves must have disappeared. A free-import country, with or without the assistance of foreign bounties, will continue to do trade with the several foreign protectionist nations long after they have ceased to do trade with one another; for in dealing with one another they confront, not only the same tariff wall which confronts us, but are hampered by the higher expenses of production which their own tariff imposes on them.

Protectionist countries (dumping or not dumping) possess no power to injure our export trade which is not exercised earlier and more injuriously upon their own trade and the trade of one another.

So long as large free or low-protected markets exist in the commercial world, this protective policy of a number of great nations, while largely restricting the volume of their export trade, could not largely reduce the volume of ours, but would chiefly operate by changing its character and direction. A rigorous protective policy pursued by all other great nations which did greatly diminish the volume of our foreign trade, could only succeed in doing so by a complete stoppage of their own foreign trade.

§ 3. In neither case is any economic force set in motion which can suck the capital out of this country into the protective countries. The attribution of such a power to protection is due to a narrow separatist view of industry. If in America or Germany a single trade, steel or cotton, gets a good deal more protection than other American or German industries, it may for a time earn an abnormally high rate of profits. In such a case it may pay English manufacturers to put up mills in the protected area, so as to share this bounty, as in a few instances has been done. It is conceivable that a large section of American or German industry, comprising (say) the great manufactures, might for a time enjoy this power to tax the other industries of America or Germany by a tariff which enabled them to raise their home prices and to earn high profits. If the mobility of capital and labour in America or Germany was so defective as to enable them to maintain these high profits, it is possible that a considerable quantity of capital and labour might flow from England into these countries. But while this is possible, it is not likely, because trades in Germany and America which were strong enough to secure this special advantage over the other industries would probably be strongly organised enough to prevent foreign capital from entering their preserves. But let us suppose certain trades or groups of trades in protective countries to possess this power to suck into their protected area some British capital. They can only accomplish this object on condition of lowering the rate of profits in other trades and exposing these trades to British competition. Protec-

tion, as we have seen, by substituting a less effective
for a more effective division of labour in a country,
reduces the average productivity of capital and
labour. If, then, that protection be so manipulated
as to secure abnormally high profits for certain
favoured trades, the effect must be to diminish
further the productivity of other industries. These
less protected industries, saddled with high expenses
of production through the general operation of the
tariff, will then be earning low profits and paying low
wages. Two results will follow. Those trades
among them which are exposed to British competition will find British goods displacing them in
neutral markets and in their own markets; these
industries will decay and British industries will
thrive at their expense. Thus Germany or America,
by the very process of drawing British capital into
a few specially favoured foreign industries, will have
improved certain other British industries employing
as much or more new capital. Though this process
might induce British capitalists to invest some capital
inside the protected areas, selecting the bounty-fed
trades, it would not cause any net reduction of
employment of capital in Great Britain. This fresh
British capital required for the expansion of trades
which were displacing German or American trades
would be furnished either by more British saving, or,
failing that, by a flow of foreign capital into Great
Britain corresponding with the flow of British capital

into the protected countries. This balance, though perhaps less regular in working than the balance of import and export trade, is equally necessary. Certain German or American trades have *ex hypothesi* drawn some British capital into these countries to share the artificial prosperity of favoured trades. But these trades are favoured primarily at the expense of other trades in their own country. These other trades, therefore, will be as much depressed as the others are prosperous. As then the prosperity of the one drew capital from Great Britain into the protected area, the depression of the other will draw capital from the protected area into Great Britain. If, as we have shown, the main burden of protection is borne by the industries of the protected country, there is no escape from this conclusion. Favoured trades can only thrive at the expense of other trades in their own country, so that any flow of capital from a free-trade country into the former must be counter-acted by a corresponding flow into the free-trade country. In point of fact, the net movement of capital must be from protective into free-trade areas, because the latter, enjoying a more productive division of labour, will have a somewhat higher profit on its capital.

The notion that a protective country, or a group of protective countries, can suck the trade out of a free-trade country depends on a fallacious generalisation from the case of single trades.

CHAPTER X

THE MYSTERY OF "DUMPING"

§ 1

"DUMPING," in the sense of selling goods for something less than "cost price," or for "whatever they will fetch," is a widely pervasive practice. Fishmongers, fruiterers, and butchers, finding themselves with a surplus of perishable goods upon their hands, offer them late on Saturday night for prices which have no definite relation to "cost." This "dumping" undoubtedly injures the ordinary local trade, for some of those who buy upon these terms would have bought a smaller quantity at ordinary prices earlier in the day were it not for the knowledge of these Saturday-night sales. Indeed, so far as the wholesale trades in perishable foods are concerned, this "dumping" policy is qualified by wholesale destruction of such portions of supply as seem likely, if an attempt is made to sell them, to spoil the market. The organised trade, having regard to the trade interest as a whole, favours destruction rather than dumping; the unorganised trade, in particular the weaker retailers, are driven by exclusive regard to their individual interests to dump their surplus. In drapery, millinery, and other trades where season and fashion are important elements, non-perishable goods are similarly "dumped" at longer intervals in "sacrifice" or "emergency" sales. Bankrupt stock is sold at prices unrelated to cost. "Summer sales" form an ever-growing practice in larger stores; goods are "marked down" to levels sometimes far below cost of production, and many customers spend a considerable part of their dress-money on these goods, who otherwise would have spent a somewhat larger sum upon smaller quantities or inferior qualities of goods in the ordinary course of trade.

Again, some shops have "leading" articles, specially low-priced classes of goods, sold cheap as an advertisement and as a means of attracting "custom."

§ 2. Now all these goods are said to be sold under cost of production. And this is true if we attribute to each unit of supply a separate cost of production. For ordinary manufacturing and commercial purposes it is doubtless convenient to base book-keeping on this estimate of separate costs. But economic analysis must, I think, take a different view. None of these classes of goods is accurately described as being sold under cost price. Even "leading" articles fetch, besides their price, a gain of general custom, the profit from which would rightly be added to their price, and, so added, would raise that price above "cost"—supposing the "attraction" to be really operative.

In the other retail cases it is evident that the goods sold at a sacrifice are a surplus due to miscalculation of demand. Such miscalculation will arise partly from the carelessness or incompetence of the trade buyers, partly to changes affecting demand so incapable of prevision that they must be regarded as chance. Tradesmen cannot afford to be found "short," for such failure to have required articles in hand not merely loses them the profit on these sales, but damages their future trade in general. In order to ensure having enough, they must run a continual risk, amounting, in some class of goods, to a certainty, of having too much. The most skilful trader must reckon on being left sometimes with a surplus which, if perishable goods, he must sell soon for what they will fetch; if non-perishable, he must similarly sell before they have become too old-fashioned. Properly regarded, these goods have no separate cost of production; he must buy them at ordinary prices and sell them below those prices, as a necessary condition of conducting his business as a whole profitably; or in other words, the loss on these "dumped" goods ensures the profitable sale of the undumped goods which form the bulk of his stock. It is only a fundamentally false way of looking at these dumped goods, taken as it were on their separate merits, that makes them appear a dead loss. Regarding them rightly, we must impute to this low-priced surplus a portion of the profit which their existence enables the normal high-priced stock to earn. Even if this surplus be the result of miscalculation, such error is a normal and indeed a necessary incident of every business. When the surplus is abnormally large, or of too-frequent recurrence, the loss incurred is to be regarded as due to general bad judgment exercised in buying, rather than as a separate loss due to the unfortunate conditions under which these particular goods must be sold. This surplus or margin, if it is no larger than is required to ensure the sound conduct of a thriving but necessarily fluctuating business, no more represents waste or loss, because it is eventually sold "below cost price," than the idle reserve which every bank must keep as a condition of being able to use the bulk of its deposits profitably. The bank reserve, it is true, fetches nothing, whereas the reserve goods of a trader are sold at some price or other. But even this apparent difference disappears when we bear in mind that the trader must always have in his stock a certain proportion of these goods, doomed to sell at (say) half their cost price; fifty per cent. of the nominal value of these goods represents at any given time a reserve or insurance fund which plays essentially the same part as a condition of the profitable conduct of his business, as the banker's reserve does in the banking business. The only difference is that he has frequently to shift the forms in which he keeps his reserve, and to dispose of the outworn forms for what he can get.

Add to this analysis the fact that in the sale of this surplus stock the trader will prefer to make, as far as possible, a separate market of them, choosing a special time for "dumping" them in large numbers, and adapting his modes of sale so as to reach a different class of purchasers from that which he normally serves.

This we see done in the Saturday-night sale, and the high-class draper will not dispose of lines of goods in which he finds himself "long" by "marking down" at ordinary times for his regular customers, but will keep them for summer sales, where a different class of customer attends to buy.

A tradesman must in the ordinary course of trade accumulate a surplus stock which he cannot dispose of in the ordinary way without spoiling the market. He generally finds it better to create a separate market for the disposal of these goods. Of course, if he is an enterprising man, or engaged in an essentially capricious trade, this "dumping" will form a larger part of his business. The larger the risks, the larger the profits and the larger the insurance.

§ 3. When we turn from retail trade to manufacture the same general analysis applies. Most manufacturers must produce on calculations of a future market; in order to make and sell at profitable prices the largest quantities of goods, they must run a normal risk of over-production. When this occurs, how shall they unload their surplus? They may try to put it on the ordinary market and let it depress prices, or they may, following the example of the shopkeeper, make some special effort to get rid of it by finding some new market for the occasion. This extraordinary market is likely to be a foreign market. There are two considerations which make it more difficult for competing manufacturers than for shop-keepers to hold in check this tendency to dumping. When a shopkeeper perceives that a line of goods is not taking, he can at once stop or curtail further purchases from the makers, but the latter cannot so easily stop or curtail their production. They have laid down special and expensive plant, have hired labour and entered contracts for the purchase of materials, etc.; they cannot change the channel of this productive energy or greatly reduce the volume of output without a very serious loss. If they are engaged in keen competition, they must be prepared to continue producing at a loss for some time, loading their former market at lower prices, forcing new markets at great sacrifices, or accumulating stock. In whatever way this surplus is disposed of there is a loss on it, if a separate cost of production be imputed to this surplus and a separate market is found for it. If it is simply thrown on to the ordinary market so as to bring down the price for the whole supply, it may cause the whole supply to be sold below cost price.

The difficulty of stopping a recognised tendency to over-production in manufacture is aggravated by the fact that a reduction of output commonly implies a more than proportionate waste of productive power, a large part of the expenses of production remaining the same for a smaller as for a larger output. The net economy of large-scale production is constantly pushing producers to maintain a maximum output in the teeth of falling prices which indicate over-stocked markets.

Indeed, this superior economy of a large output is the special source of that "dumping" which figures in international trade. If all the manufacturers in a trade acted in concert it might be more profitable for them to agree in a restriction of output, for though they would thereby produce more expensively, the margin of profit on the smaller output sold dear might be so much larger than that upon a larger output sold cheap, as to yield a net gain on their investment of capital and business energy. But where the competing manufacturers do not act in concert, it will not be profitable for any one of them to restrict his output, for he will thereby be holding up the price for the greater benefit of a competitor who does not restrict his output. So in all trades where the maximum economy of large-scale production has not been reached, there is a constant tendency among competitors to increase the output irrespective of the effects on the market. Hence a condition of trade is always liable to arise when ordinary markets are glutted, and when it may be advantageous to avoid restricting output by unloading the surplus cheaply upon distant markets. This is a temporary expedient designed to give time for a readjustment of normal output to normal demand at remunerative prices; it is employed to get rid of an actually accumulating surplus stock, to substitute a gradual for a sudden restriction, and to allow the slower normal forces regulating the distribution of industrial energy to establish a more stable equilibrium between supply and demand in the trade.

It is easy to understand how in the new conditions of world-competition in manufacture the difficulty of estimating future prices is such as to involve the frequent accumulation of surplus goods which their makers may seek to sell at a price below their "separate cost of production" in a foreign market, if by so doing they can keep up prices in the home market to a level which leaves a margin of profit. If this policy enables any net profit to be earned on the output as a whole, it is evident that this " sacrifice " on the dumped goods is an essential condition of this earning, and that to regard them as involving a dead loss, under the conditions of their sale, is not justifiable.

§ 4. So far we have treated "dumping" as it may arise under free competition of manufacturers. Apparently the earliest examples of "dumping" manufactured goods in foreign countries on any considerable scale belong to this individual business policy, as practised by English manufacturers.[1] Where manufacturers enter into concerted action for the maintenance of profitable prices, they may have recourse to two methods : they may agree to restrict their whole output, or what comes to be the same thing, not to sell any goods at less than a fixed price, or they may agree to restrict the supply for the home market, fixing a profitable price for this market, and to "dump" any surplus produce on export markets at any price or at an agreed lower price. This latter practice has been occasionally pursued for some years past by organised bodies of manufacturers in England, Germany, America, and other countries. There is no evidence that in any of these countries it has been adopted as a part of a permanent industrial policy ; it has always figured as a temporary expedient for getting rid of surplus produce without spoiling the home market.

Where the joint forces of trade combination and tariff protection give a body of manufacturers such a control of the home market as to enable them to fix highly profitable prices, this policy of "dumping" surplus goods on foreign shores becomes at once more expedient and more feasible. Under ordinary con-

[1] Cf. Professor Ashley, *The Tariff Problem*, p. 70.

K

ditions of free competition in an unprotected home
market it is, of course, possible that individual firms,
which find themselves with surplus stocks, or are producing faster than they can find a market for at
ordinary prices at home, may prefer to sell this surplus more cheaply abroad. It is, however, obvious
that, unless the home market is protected by import
duties, they cannot do this to any great extent, or
adopt it as a business policy, because, if the price at
which they sell abroad is considerably lower than the
home price, they will have to meet their own "dumped"
goods reimported and competing with them in the
home market. If dumping is regarded as anything
other than a small casual incident, it requires either
protection of the home market or closely concerted
action of the body of manufacturers in a trade, or
both, as indispensable conditions.   It seems as if both
protection and trade-organisation were necessary to
establish anything that we are entitled to call a policy
of dumping. If really free competition of a number
of producers were maintained in a protective country
such as America, it must generally pay a manufacturer better to cut down prices rather than to seek a
foreign market at a definitely lower price. This,
indeed, is what actually takes place when some improved method of production enables a number of
competing firms largely to increase their output. The
cutting of home prices down to a point of no-profit
is the direct and most urgent motive to the formation

of agreements, combinations, "trusts." Protection in the form of import duties cannot by itself form an economic foundation for a policy of dumping. Where a legal system of export bounties exists, in addition to import duties, of course dumping may become a business policy even for producers competing freely in their home market. Canada thus "dumps" iron on the British market at low prices made up to the exporters by taxes paid by the body of the Canadian people.

A combination of manufacturers or other producers, however strong, would hardly be able to maintain a policy or a repeated practice of "dumping" in foreign countries, unless they were substantially protected against the reimportation of their dumped goods. Hence we must conclude that both protection and combination are essential to a policy of dumping, *i.e.* a system of selling abroad more cheaply than at home. Where these two conditions coincide, it is at any rate theoretically possible that this discrimination of home and export prices might be systematically maintained. A German Kartel or an American trust virtually controlling their home market, might maintain a relatively high price at home, and continue to sell abroad at prices sufficiently lower to enable them to dispose of the rest of their regular output. It is important to recognise clearly this theoretic basis of dumping, not merely as a casual expedient for dealing with over-supply, but as a possible permanent business policy.

§ 5. Some who will easily recognise that it is not right to impute a separate cost to the margin or surplus required to ensure a trade, or to some casual surplus which it is best to sacrifice, refuse to admit that it can conceivably pay a trust or a group of protected manufacturers to sell abroad a regular part of their output at a price which would involve a net loss if all their output were sold at this price.

The theoretical feasibility of such a policy can be best demonstrated by hypothetical figures. A mill running at its full capacity can turn out 900 tons per diem at a cost of (say) 17*s*. per ton ; running at two-thirds capacity it turns out 600 tons at (say) 19*s*. per ton. Assuming that the same market price 25*s*. could be got for the 900 tons as for the 600 tons, the profit on the full working would be (900 × 8*s*.) 7,200 shillings, or £360 per diem, as compared with the profit on a two-thirds working at (600 × 6*s*.) 3,600 shillings, or £180 per diem. It is, however, evident that the same price cannot be got for the 900 tons as for the 600. It is quite possible that if 600 tons could be put on the market at 25*s*. per ton, thus yielding a net profit of 6s. per ton or £180 on the output, 900 might bring down the price as low as 19s. per ton, yielding a net profit of only 2*s*. per ton or £90 on the output. But if it can be arranged to separate the protected home market and the foreign market, and to sell 600 tons in the former at 25*s*. per ton, and 300 tons in the latter at a dumping price of even 16s. (less than "cost" price on the full output), the profits on the 600 tons would be (600 × 8s.) 4,800 shillings or £240, the loss on the 300 "dumped" tons would be 300 shillings or £15. The total output of 900 tons would thus fetch a profit of £240 – £15, or £225. The so-called loss of £15 on the "dumped" portion of the output is the condition of earning 8s. per ton profit as compared with 6s. per ton on the 600 tons sold in the home market.

This possible economy rests on the so-called law of increasing returns, or, in other words, on the fact that a large part of the expenses of production is relatively fixed, increasing much more slowly than the increase of output.

§ 6. Thus it is quite clear that a trust or other non-competing group in a protected country might conceivably find the technical economy of producing on the larger scale permitted by an export trade so great, that it would pay them, as a continuous business policy, to supply a foreign market at what appears to be "below cost price." There are various ways in which this low export price may be regarded. It may be said that the real or true economic price for the whole output lies between the artificially high home price and the artificially low export price, the home consumers, in fact, paying part of the true price for the foreign consumer. This correctly describes what happens: the home consumer subsidises the foreign consumer.

Or we may treat the export goods as a by-product in relation to the home products; the latter can only be economically produced on condition that the former are also produced, and once produced it is better to sell them for what they will fetch, like a pure by-product. A by-product is not considered to have any cost price, certainly no separate cost price can be imputed to it. So with these dumped export goods, they may be considered as having no true cost price. But it will presently appear that they cannot strictly be treated as pure by-products, because the price they fetch does affect the question whether they shall be produced or how many of them shall be produced. The truth is, that this phenomenon of dumping is the most convincing exposure of the economic fallacy of imputing to any portion of an output a *separate* cost of production. The true formula runs thus: If 1,000 tons be produced, each ton costs 10s.; if 2,000 tons be produced, each ton costs 8s.; if 5,000 tons, 7s., and so on. But if the cost of a ton always depends upon the number of other tons produced along with it, a ton can never be rightly regarded as a separate economic unit with a separate cost attached to it. It is only the whole output that has a true cost. The business man who handles this output for the market, though he has to sell it in pieces, will not consider that he must sell each piece so as to make a separate profit on its proportion of cost of production to that of the whole output; he will aggregate the prices he gets for the several portions of the output and treat this aggregate as one price, just as he treated the aggregate cost as one cost. He will always consider the effect of a separate sale upon his market as a whole, recognising the utility of discriminating prices both in home and foreign markets so as to secure the largest aggregate profits. He will, of course, also consider the details of the separate sales, refusing to sell certain goods below a certain price, not ultimately because this price is "below cost," but because it is so cheap as to react unprofitably upon the aggregate net profits, or even to affect injuriously the sale of future outputs. In a word, excepting where what is called the law of Constant Returns prevails, *i.e.* where there is no net technical advantage in producing a larger or a smaller output, there is nothing that can be rightly called a separate cost of production for units of output.

The fact that discrimination of prices takes place in disposing of an output does not therefore warrant us, in serious economic analysis, in attributing a separate profit or loss to each portion by comparing the price got with a separate cost attributed to its production. It is, then, an established economic possibility that a non-competing group or interest, in a protected country, might find it profitable as a lasting policy to sell goods abroad at a price definitely lower than they could there be produced with equal capital, skill, and industrial knowledge. Or it might find it profitable only occasionally to resort to this method of disposing of a surplus. Or, finally, it might "dump" cheap goods in order to break down the home trade in a foreign country, with the object of capturing the foreign market and then raising prices.

To either of the latter two practices the especial economy of large-scale production which we have just considered is not essential; we have seen that in retail trade resort is had to getting rid of a casual surplus by selling it for what it will fetch in a distant market, while the policy of selling cheap for a while in order to break a competitor and capture a market is common throughout the world of commerce. The trust or non-competing group in a protected country is, however, in a stronger position to utilise either of these policies than are other producers.

§ 7. Before considering the case of a permanent policy of discriminating prices, it will be well to discuss the feasibility and the desirability of using import duties as a means of counteracting these sorts of "dumping."

Dumping as a means of disposing of a temporary surplus has been shown to be a general practice. Is there any sufficient reason to distinguish foreign from domestic dumping and to provide against it by tariff enactment? The question is one, not of economic principle, but of economic and political expediency. Casual dumping of indigestible surplus products cannot be lightly dismissed as a mere "bonus" of the foreigner to the British consumer. It is that, but it is something more. It is a sudden blow to the stability of a British trade, falling at a time when it is likely to prove more than usually injurious. For there exists sufficient unity and sympathy throughout the industrial world to render it likely that surplus production in America or Germany, whether due to slackness of demand or to improved methods of production, will be accompanied by a similar condition of British trade. "Dumping" attributable to this cause will therefore come when it does most harm to a trade already suffering from, or threatened with, over-production. The shock of this injury disorganising a whole trade may be very inadequately compensated by a temporary cheapness of prices to the consumer. Even when the dumped goods which form the finished product of our British industry are the raw materials of another, as has happened with the dumping of coke, pig-iron, steel-plates, etc., it does not follow that this boom of one trade and slump of another yield a net benefit to British industry, as compared with the maintenance of normal conditions of stability or progress. Indeed, it is impossible to avoid the conclusion that these miraculous sudden interventions from outside are demoralising incidents, breaking confidence in the regular order of economic nature. Were "dumping" adopted by a foreign trust or combination as a means of invading our markets, underselling British producers in order to capture the trade and afterwards to raise prices to a "profitable" level, such attacks directed against important British industries from behind protective tariff walls might cause great distress. It is, of course, true that the fears sometimes entertained of an organised attack against all or most of our staple trades which should ruin British industry as a whole is not merely a wild exaggeration, but involves a misunderstanding of the nature of industry. It would be impossible even for an organised conspiracy of several "dumping" nations bent on injuring British trade to destroy our trade as a whole or even to diminish its volume. Such a notion presupposes that there only exists a fixed limited number of trades which, judiciously attacked, would all succumb, leaving not a wrack behind. In point of fact, unless the confederacy of dumpers were prepared to "keep" the entire British nation as consumers by free subsidies of all manner of commodities, the attempt to take some British trades could only drive British industry into other trades, an ever-increasing proportion of British capital and labour passing into the production of such perishable goods and such services as did not lend themselves to dumping. Let foreign nations "dump" food, clothing, and all forms of portable convenience and luxury upon us, refusing to take British goods and services in payment; we should be driven to the most magnificent development of housing, transport and all distributive services, public and private, to the amplest cultivation of the professions and the fine arts; the rest of this bounty we should take out in leisure, a broader margin to our national life.

While then the graver apprehensions of the possible effects of dumping are manifestly absurd, the incidental effects of a more fragmentary policy might be serious enough to deserve public attention. While "dumping" as a weapon could not destroy or permanently reduce the size of our domestic industry as a whole, it might do considerable harm by disturbance and dislocation. Directed with more cunning, it might even harm our trade worse than the casual dumping to get rid of surpluses. If it were feasible to prevent such dumping by prohibitive or protective import duties, such action would offend no sane principle of free exchange.

It is entirely a question of expediency. If a tariff could be arranged which would act promptly where it was needed, for just as long as it was needed, and as far as it was needed, there could be no sound objection to its application. The difficulties are purely practical. But they are so grave as to be almost insuperable. The "dumping" we have described is essentially a sudden process, it is, or can be, conducted with considerable secrecy, and would be extremely difficult to distinguish from a normal decline of prices due to a normal increase of imports. It is seldom possible to lay one's fingers on any stock of goods entering our ports and to say with reasonable confidence, "These are dumped." A considerable degree of secrecy is now observed in selling abroad at lower prices; if it were necessary to meet a fiscal weapon, this secrecy would become impenetrable. Either some official must be empowered to deal with emergency cases, and with the constant false alarms which interested home producers will be ever raising in their eagerness to keep out foreign goods ; or else a "sliding scale" of the most intricate character and subject to continual revision must be applied to every trade where foreign competition presses. To entrust so serious a sudden power either to the discretion of officials or to the mechanical precision of sliding scales will appear the more perilous the closer one reflects upon the details of these operations. Were the powerful trusts of America and Germany, with the express assistance of their governments, publicly to plan attacks upon our staple metal, textile, and shipbuilding trades, by the instrument of dumping, so grave an emergency might warrant the use of the tariff as a weapon, and its adoption would be nowise derogatory to the principles of free exchange. But for smaller emergencies it would assuredly be safer to bear the blow than to put the clumsy and ineffectual weapons of import duties into the hands of imperfectly wise officials.

But this is mainly a question of politics rather than of economic theory. If an official were wise enough and a good enough tariff could he constructed, a nation would be quite justified in thus warding off dumped goods which did more harm by disorganising trade than good by a temporary lowering of prices.

§ 8. The hypothetical case of a continuous policy of dumping, not to dispose of a temporary surplus or primarily to capture a market, but in order to practise most profitably large-scale production, involves different considerations. If we in England could rely upon receiving a fairly constant large supply of boots, sheet-iron or steam engines from America at prices below those for which we could produce them, ought the mere fact that this dumping is supported by a foreign tariff, or even by an export bounty, to induce us to refuse them or to place a tariff on them? True, the beginning of this policy may break down a British industry, but if the policy is to be a continuous one, the benefit to the consumer, and in many instances to other trades where these dumped goods are raw materials, will obviously outweigh this single temporary blow. It will be better to accept this damage to a British trade in the same spirit in which we should accept imports which undersold our products by superior use of machinery, or better natural resources. Acting in our own interests as a nation, it would be folly to attempt to distinguish between a cheapness which is the result respectively of " fair " and " unfair " competition, provided that cheapness is permanent. Unless, therefore, we are prepared to protect all British industries against all foreign competition, there can be no reason to put an import duty upon bounty-fed foreign goods where there is any reasonable security of a continuance of the bounty.

§ 9. It remains briefly to consider the economic efficacy of taxing dumped goods as a means of revenue. We have spoken of "dumped goods" as being sold "for whatever they would fetch." If this were strictly true, it follows that an import tax imposed on them would not cause a rise of price, but would be borne entirely by the producers. Such an *ad valorem* tax might conceivably take 80 per cent. of the selling value of the goods without causing the dumper to check his dumping. In such a case the British producer would be nowise "protected," but the British revenue would be a gainer.

This, however, is not what would happen. Though "dumped goods" cannot be said to have any separate cost of production, the price at which they are dumped is not "any" price, but one calculated to dispose of such quantity of output as will, by keeping down the aggregate cost of production and raising the aggregate returns for sales, yield the greatest total profit. Any considerable *ad valorem* duty would disturb this maximum profit by reducing the returns from the export trade. The effect of such an import duty will depend upon the relation of the former price of the dumped goods to the normal British price. It may have paid the dumper to dump a comparatively small amount which forced a market at a price just below the normal British price. Or the economy of large production might have made it more profitable to "dump" a larger quantity, so bringing down the selling price far below the normal British price. The effect of an *ad valorem* tax on dumped goods will differ in the two cases. In the former case, the tax will lie almost entirely on the dumper, if he continues to dump at all. For if he were to dump a smaller quantity, thus sacrificing something in economy of production by reducing the total output, he could not recoup himself by raising the prices for his dumped exports, because the former price was fixed just below the British competitive price. He must therefore either cease dumping, or pay the entire tax out of his pocket, continuing to dump as before. In the latter event the British Treasury has succeeded in taxing the monopoly profit of the protected American producers.

If, however, the dumping price has been fixed low, so as to take off a large surplus product, the effect of an import duty will be to reduce the quantity of dumping, a smaller quantity being sold at a higher price. This rise of price cannot be high enough to compensate fully the loss to the "dumper" of reducing his output and so producing more expensively, but it will furnish some compensation. The incidence of the import duty will then be divided between the British consumer and the American producer; in what proportion it is impossible to predict, for it will depend upon the reaction of reduced output on cost of production and the reaction of reduced supply on demand, or more strictly speaking, upon the relation between these two reactions.

§ 10. In the case of "casual" dumping, then, protection by import duties would be virtually inefficacious; such duties would be too slow of operation and too uncertain of effect. In the case of "aggressive" dumping, in order to "steal" a market, it would only be possible to take effective action by import duties in cases where publicity attached to the invasion. In the case of the steady maintenance of a policy of low export prices, the gain to the consumer and to other trades in the country where such goods are "dumped" will normally outweigh the damage done by a temporary displacement of capital and labour in a single British trade. It might, however, be a sound revenue policy to impose an import duty which, levied on goods produced under conditions enabling them to assist in earning monopoly profits for a foreign "trust" or "combination," would fall entirely, or in large part, upon the producer.

Monopoly profits directly taxed cannot transfer

the tax ; and even an import tax, the only way in which a foreigner can reach them, may sometimes succeed in lying on them sufficiently to make the experiment a profitable one for the revenue.

There is, however, no evidence of the practice of such a regular system of low-price exportation by trusts and other combinations as would render any such taxation deserving of present consideration. The dumping of goods by American trusts and German Kartels during recent years is proved to rest on no organised system of maintaining a cheap export trade, but is adopted merely as a temporary expedient for getting rid of a casual surplus, In a few instances cheap export prices have been adopted by enterprising foreign firms as an attempt to capture the British or other markets. Nowhere has there been developed a system of regular bounty-fed export trade under conditions which would enable us profitably to apply an import duty as a safe instrument of revenue.

L

CHAPTER XI

PROTECTION AS A REMEDY FOR UNEMPLOYMENT

§ 1

PROTECTION claims to secure fuller employ- ment and higher remuneration for capital and labour. The difficulty felt by many classes of in- vestors in finding safe profitable uses for their money, by business managers in keeping plant and machinery fully occupied, by workmen in obtaining regular employment, is a constant and a serious trouble. The common explanation of the *laissez- faire* economist, imputing this unemployment of a "margin" of spare capital and labour as a sound necessary condition of the elasticity of modern industry, or as an equally necessary result of in- herent irregularities of certain trades, does not convince. The quantity and character of the waste are too grave to warrant the acceptance of this fatalistic interpretation of "un"- and "under"-em- ployment. Frequently recurring periods of bad trade exhibit the simultaneous waste of all the factors of production; this waste is greater than is required for the normal processes of industrial adaptation. These larger wastes of unemployment are most patent in countries which have entered the era of mechanical industry, and which experience an ever-growing difficulty in finding markets wherein to dispose of their maximum output. As more countries have developed machinery for manufacture and transport, the condition of the industrial world has become one in which it always appears more difficult to sell than to buy. Now the general principles of exchange furnish no adequate solution of this difficulty. A sale of goods for money is merely one-half of the complete exchange of commodities for commodities which is the sole end of commerce; why should this half be more difficult than the other half? The bland assumption that money, or general purchasing power, is naturally preferred to the possession of any single class of goods merely begs the question. If every producer were morally certain that he could find a buyer for his goods at the present market price, he would feel no such anxiety as he now commonly experiences; he would be no more eager to sell than the purchaser to buy. It is his well-grounded belief that in ordinary times the supply of the goods he offers exceeds, or may at any time exceed, the demand at current prices that prompts his anxiety to sell. Now this accepted tendency of supply to outrun demand is a paradox. Since the whole object of production is consumption, and since with every increase of production is born a corresponding power of consumption, why should there be exhibited this chronic tendency to over-production, congestion of the machinery of production, slackening or stoppage of the machinery, and corresponding waste of capital and labour by unemployment or under-employment? The frequent attempt to explain the booms and slumps of actual industry by references to the financial or book-keeping side of trade, in which " over-confidence " and subsequent collapse of " credit," essentially subjective conditions, are dragged into the chain of objective events as explanations of over-production and industrial collapse, adds new confusion to a complicated matter. " Over-confidence " and " collapse of credit " are but financial reflections of objective industrial facts in relation to quantities of production and consumption of commodities ; they are never independent forces or prime causes. If a general fall of prices occurs, accompanied by a slackening of the pace of production, i.e. unemployment, the only efficient cause of these phenomena is a refusal of the industrial community to take out of the industrial machine, in their capacity of consumers, as much as they put into the machine in their capacity of producers. In fact, over-production (as distinguished from misproduction, which is a regular necessary waste) only arises from under-consumption, a refusal of the community to make full use of its consuming power so as to keep fully employed the factors of production.

§ 2. Since the only rational inducement to produce is the desire to consume, we have to find an explanation for the failure of the latter force to function properly, in defective demand for commodities. The possibility of a congestion of the machinery of general production is only intelligible on the supposition that a part of the power to demand goods for present consumption is withheld by some who have the power to consume. The refusal of a full application of the power to purchase and consume is itself only explicable as part of the wider phenomenon of maldistribution of wealth in modern societies.

In a well-ordered society, where distribution of wealth as consuming power was proportioned either to the efforts or the needs of the producers, every increase in the powers of production of the community would automatically be attended by a corresponding rise in the general standard of consumption, effective demand rising to correspond with every increased power of supply. Only where this just "natural" distribution of consuming power exists is there any security that consumption rising with every increase of production will keep taut the reins of industry, and render unemployment or waste of capital and labour, beyond the needs of normal readjustment, impossible. If, on the other hand, inequality of economic opportunities is such as to impose a grave inequality in the distribution of wealth, some classes getting a power of purchase greater than is required to supply legitimate and pressing needs, other classes getting a power of purchase insufficient to satisfy their needs, we have an economic condition which explains the paradox of over-production, under-consumption, and unemployment. The growth of illegitimate or "luxurious" needs is not such as to give an adequate stimulus to the full use of very large incomes in demand for commodities; from such incomes emanates a great amount of automatic saving, implying a corresponding refusal to demand commodities.[1] The irregularity thus introduced into industry obliges other classes of more moderate wealth to secure themselves against anticipated collapses of income by setting aside and saving a larger percentage of their current incomes than would otherwise be saved. From these causes the inequality of distribution of wealth issues in an over-saving on the part of the community, *i.e.* a saving of a larger proportion of the current income than is

---

[1] The contention that "saving" involves a demand for other sorts of goods, *e.g.* capital goods, and causes as much production and employment as "spending," is only true so far as the first effect goes. Ultimately over-saving can be shown to check production. A full argument upon this point, here impossible, is presented in the author's *The Problem of the Unemployed.* (Methuen.)

economically required to assist in the production of sufficient goods to supply current or prospective consumption.

This over-saving seems to be a natural product of maldistribution of wealth, implies superfluous forms of capital which, when put into productive operation with labour, cause over-production and the congestion of markets, which is the preliminary to under-production or unemployment.

§ 3. If this analysis is correct, unemployment can arise only from bad distribution of income, and can be cured only by a better distribution, *i.e.* by means which place an increased proportion of the general income in the hands of the classes which will use it for the demand for commodities. A greater equalisation of incomes, by cancelling or reducing the "unearned increments" which pass to the rich in the form of "rents," monopoly profits, or excessive salaries, and by raising the wages of the labouring classes, which will be spent in securing a higher standard of comfort,[1] is the only effective provision against unemployment of capital and labour.

This brief analysis of a difficult subject is essential, because it furnishes a true test for the claims of protectionists to cure unemployment. If Protection is

---

[1] There is, of course, no reason why a working class, having raised its standard of current consumption to the full maintenance of family efficiency, should not contribute its share to the "saving" of the community required to maintain the sufficient growth of capital.

to increase the general volume of employment, and not merely to stimulate certain trades by depressing others, it can only do so on condition of increasing the share of the general income which goes to the wage-earning and lower middle classes.

§ 4. Now the advocates of a protectionist policy have seldom claimed this result, nor have they admitted the application of this economic test. The conflict of argument between protectionist and free trader upon the "unemployment" issue has, in fact, been inconclusive and even futile, precisely because both contestants have ignored the only reasonable criterion of improved employment, viz. a rising standard of consumption.

Both parties have commonly resorted to single concrete cases or to the effects upon individual trades, which are fallacious modes of argument. The futility of such a discussion may be illustrated by a single instance. The London County Council orders for its tramways a quantity of steel rails from Belgium because it can buy them there 20 per cent. cheaper than in England. The protectionist objects, on the ground that though the rails would have cost more if bought at Leeds, this extra cost would be far more than compensated by the net increase of employment afforded to English capital and labour. The free trader replies that no more employment is given to English capital and labour by buying the rails in Leeds than by buying them in Belgium, because if we bought them in Leeds we should not produce the goods which would be exported to pay for them if they came from Belgium. The protectionist replies, "It is true we should not export these goods to Belgium, but they (or their equivalent) would be produced in England all the same : instead of being sent in export trade to pay Belgium, they would go to Leeds to pay for the same rails produced there. The net result is that as the result of refusing the Belgian tender and buying in his own country, more is produced and more is consumed in England." The free trader may point out that the production of the steel rails in England is *ex hypothesi* more expensive, and involves a larger employment of capital and labour than if bought from Belgium, and that this excess in expenditure on rails involves a corresponding reduction in expenditure on other articles which are made in England. In the case taken, this reduction on other articles amounts to 20 per cent. of the expense of the rails. "But even allowing this," the protectionist replies, "the result of buying the rails in Leeds is that 80 per cent. of the expenditure employs additional British capital and labour."

So far the argument has not assumed the operation of a tariff. But suppose a tariff, imposed for the purpose of inducing the County Council to buy Leeds instead of Belgian rails, enabled the Leeds firm to raise its prices beyond the free-trade price by

20 per cent. or more. Even then, it is contended by the protectionist, 60 per cent. of the price paid for British rails represents employment which would have been lost, without compensation in other trades, if the order had gone to Belgium. Now this protectionist conclusion, though the free trader commonly haggles at accepting it, is correct. But what does it amount to? Simply this, that there exists in most trades, at most times, a margin of productive power in capital and labour not fully employed; so an order placed in England, instead of going abroad, is in ordinary times capable of execution without calling for any capital and labour to be diverted from any other employment, as the free trader commonly insists must happen. The real fallacy which underlies the argument is the supposition that because the existence of a margin of unutilised capital and labour makes it possible to get a single additional order executed more expensively in England without diverting capital and labour from other employments, this process can be enlarged indefinitely, and can be made the profitable basis of a fiscal system, which shall divert whole trades from the Continent into England, or keep them in England when otherwise they would have gone abroad. The necessary margin required for elasticity of business can be trenched upon for the execution of a single or a few extra orders, but it cannot contain the reserve productive power for a new large trade obtained by preference.

This seems so obvious, that one is driven to ask how it can appear possible for employment to be artificially created for English trades by preferential or protective methods without seeming to cause a diversion of capital and labour from other more productive employments into the newly subsidised trades. If every trade or most trades were normally in the condition supposed by those economists who scout the possibility of "general over-production," the margin of productive energy in a given trade must be a very small proportion of the whole, and it would appear quite impossible to divert foreign orders to British firms through a tariff, without depleting other British industries of their capital and labour to increase the productive power of the favoured trades.

But if we once admit the possibility of that larger margin or excess of productive power which is proved to exist, not in a few trades, but in most trades, during periods of slackness or depression, we begin to comprehend the true underlying source of the plausibility of protection. The protectionist says, if he understands his case, " You are right in urging that if we stop the imports which compete with our own products, we must stop the export trade which pays for them ; but you are wrong in arguing that the goods which represented that export trade will cease to be produced, for they will be wanted to remunerate the British capital and labour which make the goods formerly imported : moreover, you are wrong in saying that capital and labour must be diverted from other industries to make these goods ; the stoppage of the imports has led to the employ- ment of British capital and labour which previously represented an unnecessary waste." The practical business man is likely to be impressed by this argu- ment, because he is well aware that in assuming the existence in ordinary times of a considerable margin of unemployed energy of capital and labour in most trades, the protectionist correctly describes the actual conditions of modern industry.

§ 5. The real case for protection, as I understand it, rests upon this assumption, that in normal times there does exist, not the smallest margin of capital and labour needed for current trade adjustments, but an amount considerably larger than this, and that, if a tariff can be framed to substitute the employment of this productive energy for that of foreign capital and labour, the volume of our production will be greater. It may, indeed, be objected that more British capital and labour is required to produce the product than the foreign capital and labour which formerly produced it, and that, to pay the higher price thus caused, some consuming power must be diverted from other applications, with the result of causing unemployment in these other industries. But on the hypothesis of the existence of a con- siderable suplus-producing power, this new unemployment will be much less than that which has been supplied with work, so that a net increase of British employment will result.

The protective policy, in this analysis, appears to have transferred a certain amount of employment from foreign capital and labour to British capital and labour, not, indeed, appreciably altering the total amount of unemployment in the industrial world, but reducing the proportion of this waste which falls on British industry.

It is the theoretic possibility of filling this hole of unemployment by an artificial diversion of trade through protection that gives what plausibility attaches to a tariff. It might be a profitable economic policy for a nation to pay a slightly higher price for certain consumable commodities, and by reducing to a corresponding extent its demand for other commodities to displace capital and labour in these industries, if the result were to secure full regular employment for considerable quantities of capital and labour which would otherwise be wasted.

But between this theoretic service of protection and a practically serviceable tariff there is a great gulf fixed. For it must be borne in mind that the theoretic validity of this remedy for unemployment rests wholly on the hypothesis that there exists a considerable margin of spare available power of capital and labour, an unemployed margin beyond the legitimate needs of ordinary business adjustments, and that, therefore, orders diverted from the foreigner could be executed without causing capital and labour to leave employments where they were more productively engaged.

But it is impossible to know how large this margin is in any given trade at any time, and any tariff which stimulated a British industry beyond the limit of this margin would cause grave injury, by diverting capital and labour already productively employed to a less productive employment. Since the logic of protection constantly drives in the direction of greater stringency and wider extension, it would be impossible to restrict a tariff to a certain carefully measured protection for certain trades; trades already protected would demand more protection, other trades at first unprotected would clamour for protection, and no effective stand could be made against either sort of pressure.

Talk of the application of a " scientific " tariff is illusory; the ever-changing conditions of commerce and of the industrial arts render delicate " scientific" forecasts impossible, and when the interests of a trade are strongly engaged in producing an impression, and in supporting that impression by apparently substantial evidence, they will always get the better of the " scientific" expert. Their art will conquer his science. Their strong self-interest will overpower his weaker guardianship of the further interest. This is inevitable. The two instances where we have admitted the theoretic validity of protective measures are open to this perversion in a peculiar degree. The first is the case of a tax on foreign goods dumped on our shores with the object of damaging our home industry, seizing our market, and then raising prices. This tax we found might be economically efficacious and politically advisable, if it could be correctly imposed. But we found that the proof of evil intention, which is the condition of the application of this remedy, would be well-nigh impossible; the British industry seeking protection could hardly ever bring direct evidence of intention on the part of foreigners, and would be virtually confined to providing evidence of mere under-selling, due possibly to better economy of production or of discrimination between home and export prices, not in itself an injury to the recipients of this bounty.

The second instance of theoretically valid protection is the case we have here under discussion. When we turn from the general and theoretic to the individual and concrete, we find ourselves confronted with similarly insuperable difficulties. A British trade competing with foreign imports is losing ground; it cannot get sufficient orders to keep its capital and labour fully occupied. British orders are going to foreign firms; a good many mills are closed or working half time; many workmen are on the unemployed list. Here is a case where it seems feasible by a tariff on imports to secure an increase of the aggregate of employment for Great Britain in accordance with our analysis. But this assistance is only valid on two conditions : first, that the additional work thus secured can be executed by the unemployed margin without trenching on capital and labour usefully engaged elsewhere ; secondly, that the industry thus helped is not a decaying industry. This last point requires further elucidation. Some British industries will at any given time be growing rapidly and absorbing more capital and labour ; others will be virtually stationary, their capital and labour sometimes fully occupied, sometimes not, according to the general condition of trade ; a few industries may be actually declining, either because of a definite superiority of some foreign industry, or from change in fashion affecting demand, or because they are displaced from their position in the export cargo of Great Britain by other commodities. If any of these causes is operative it signifies a natural decline of a British industry necessary and desirable in the interests of British industry as a whole ; the trade is not worth maintaining in its former shape and size. Now such a genuinely decaying industry will necessarily show a large quantity of unemployed capital and labour. The social utility has in reality gone out of this ; the forms of capital should be left to die, and the labour should be assisted to find other employment as quickly as possible. To support such an industry by means of a tariff would be a public injury, impeding the wholesome processes of internal readjustment in the industry of the nation. But if a tariff were once admitted as a remedy for unemployment, it would certainly be abused for the support of these decaying industries. It would be practically impossible in most instances for officials to determine between true decline and the conditions which we have designated as an excessive margin of unemployment.

§ 7. When to these genuine difficulties of discrimination we add the political abuses rampant under tariff legislation, the case against the use of a scientific tariff as a remedy for "unemployment" becomes overwhelming. Nowhere in tariff legislation or administration can "science" or "theory" hold its own against the political "pull" of industrial interests. In the United States the "scientific theory" is that the tariff should be so arranged as to protect American capital and labour against the competition of cheaper European production by equalising the expenses of production in Europe and America.

But it is not seriously pretended that the tariff is actually designed to conform to this idea. The plasticity of a tariff law in process of construction is such that it reflects much less the economic needs than the political power of the various in-

M

dustries.[1] Nor is this peculiar to the United States. The development of tariff legislation in European countries, irrespective of this form of government, illustrates the same inherent tendency. In "scientific" Germany and in "theoretic" France there is almost as little regard shown to principles in the making of tariffs as in the United States.

The attitude habitually and everywhere adopted by organised industries and by individual business men towards government wherever its functions affect business life is utterly opposed to the idea of a dispassionate scientific fiscal policy. There is no

---

[1] The following passage from the work of an American protectionist writer, Mr. A. S. Bolles, describes the process of making the 1883 tariff:—

"The history of tariff-making is not particularly honourable in all its details to any party or interest. It has too often partaken of a personal fight by manufacturers against the public and each other. The struggle on this occasion before Congress lasted nearly the whole session. . . . The iron ore producers desired a tariff of 85 cents a ton on ore ; the steel rail makers were opposed to the granting of more than 50 ; the manufacturers of fence wire were opposed to an increase of duty on wire rods used for making wire, and favoured a reduction ; the manufacturers of rods in this country were desirous of getting an increase ; the manufacturers of floor oilcloths desired a reduction or abolition of the duty on the articles used by them ; the soap manufacturers desired the putting of caustic soda on the free list, which the American manufacturers of it opposed ; some of the woollen manufacturers were desirous that protection should be granted to the manufacturers of dyestuffs, and some were not ; the manufacturers of tanned foreign goat and sheep skins desired the removal of the tariff on such skins ; those who tanned them, and who were much less numerous, were equally tenacious in maintaining the tariff on the raw skins ; and the same conflict arose between other interests."—*Financial History of the United States* (1861–85), pp. 479–80.

trade and but few men who would refrain from bringing influence to bear on government in order to secure a public contract, to evade the pressure of a proposed tax, or to obtain an import duty on their own article of manufacture. While this remains true, it would be wanton folly to entrust a government with the formation and administration of a tariff professedly confined to the attainment of a few special, delicate, theoretically valid defences of British trade. The certain harm would greatly outweigh the possible gain.

§ 8. Moreover, reverting to economic theory, protection, regarded as a remedy for unemployment, is the substitution of a bad palliative for a cure. A palliative is good if it is a stop-gap which does not impede the operation of genuinely curative forces; it is bad if it does impede them. Now we have seen that the industrial disease termed "unemployment" arises directly from under-consumption, and that under-consumption is traceable to undesirable inequality in the distribution of wealth. Therefore the only really "scientific" remedy is one which will raise the standard of consumption, thus expanding naturally the volume of employment of capital and labour. Protection is a bad palliative, because it does not increase the capacity of consumption to keep pace with production. Even could protection be rigorously restricted to the narrow limits where it has been found to be theoretically defensible, it would do nothing to redress the balance of distribution in favour of expenditure as against over-saving. The slight increase of the aggregate of consumption it secured would be attended by a more than proportionate increase of production, if we assume that the proportions of rents, profits, and wages are the same in the protected trades as in other trades. In point of fact, it would be easy to show that such protection, like all protection, will profit landowners and capitalists more than labourers, and thus make for an increased maldistribution of the general income, which will cause increased over-saving, over-production, depression, and unemployment. This would happen under a really scientific tariff confined to objects theoretically defensible. But if we take the net results of any actual tariff adopted to "protect" the business interests of Great Britain or the British Empire, the injury would be far graver and more far-reaching.

That a protective tariff, however devised, furnishes no effective remedy for unemployment is proved in practice by the fact that the high-tariff countries are liable to depressions of trade at least as frequent and as wasteful of capital and labour as the free-import countries.

§ 9. Indeed, it is not difficult to perceive how a general system of protection, designed to safeguard the national industry against the competition of imports, must aggravate the conditions which are responsible for unemployment. Every fresh barrier against freedom of exchange, rendering less effective the division of labour among nations, causes the capital and labour in the country which imposes it to be less productively employed than it would otherwise have been. Thus the aggregate of actual wealth produced in the country is diminished. This reduction of real income will not be borne equally or proportionately by the various classes that contribute to production. A duty upon imported agricultural produce, raising the price of food and stimulating British agriculture, will give a larger rent to the landowners. Land which was formerly below the margin of cultivation will now yield a rent, and the rent of each acre of land which formerly paid rent will be raised. Taking wheat land for our example, we may conclude that a larger proportion of the increased aggregate of wheat grown will be paid as rent, and that the exchange value of each quarter of this wheat as compared with commodities and services not equally protected will rise. Hence the landowners reap a double gain, taking not merely a larger proportion of the national income than before, but an absolute increase of wealth out of a diminished aggregate. Thus a smaller proportion of the diminished national income remains for the remuneration of capital and labour. Is it reasonable to suppose that this loss will fall most heavily on capital? When we remember that one of the inevitable consequences of protection is to facilitate combinations of capital in the form of syndicates and trusts, and that these powerful corporations will be able to exercise influence in the moulding of tariffs, it becomes evident that the capitalist industries which are largest, best-equipped, and most profitably worked will use the tariff to secure for themselves further advantages. In a country which protects agriculture and manufactures, the landowners and the great capitalists must gain by the tariff. Experience shows that they are the only gainers. Capital embarked on smaller, feebler industries does not get its share of protection, nor can it make such effective use of what it possesses to secure monopoly; the other great industries, not exposed to foreign competition, and so not "protected," suffer in the exchange value of their commodities as compared with the artificially raised values of the protected commodities; the internal transport trades, the distributing classes, the professions, and last and most, the wage-earning members of the nation, are losers. Labour loses trebly: first, through the diminution of the average of its productivity due to the impaired division of labour; next, through its reduced capacity for bargaining with capital, now more strongly organised in trusts and combines; and finally, through the enhanced prices of commodities, which tell more heavily on the workers than upon the wealthier classes, because their expenditure upon food and other highly protected goods is greater in proportion to their income than that of the wealthy.

Of a diminished aggregate income, resulting from protection, a larger proportion goes to the land-owning and the capitalist employers in the protected manufactures. The other classes suffer ; employers and investors in the unprotected or low-protected manufactures, the transport and distributive trades, suffer through enhanced expenses of production and a fall in the purchasing power of their profits ; the professions, the public services, the entire body of the salaried and wage-earning classes suffer through a rise of prices, which they are unable fully to counteract by a corresponding rise of money income.

§ 10. This loss, due to the diminished productivity of the national industry under protection, will not, of course, fall equally upon the losing classes ; in proportion to their economic strength as bargainers, and their power of effective combination, they will succeed in recouping themselves for enhanced expenses and higher prices of commodities by raising the prices of the goods or services they sell, and thus throwing the stress of the burden of protection upon the classes who are weaker and less effective in bargaining. The small manufacturers, the struggling traders, the lowest-salaried officials and clerks, the lowest-skilled, worst-paid, manual labourers will sustain the heaviest loss. Their loss will be heaviest in two senses. They will, on the one hand, be least capable of pressing for a rise of money wage to compensate the higher cost of living ; on the other hand, since their former standard of living was the lowest, any reduction of that standard causes more actual misery and inflicts a greater injury upon their economic efficiency than in the case where a higher " standard " has hitherto obtained. Thus a protective tariff upon agricultural and manufactured imports, benefiting most the wealthiest classes of the community, injuring most the poorest grades of workers, alters for the worse the distribution of wealth. It increases " rents," surplus profits, and other " unearned increment " of the incomes of the wealthy classes, while it reduces the income of the working classes. Now our earlier analysis disclosed the fact that maldistribution of wealth, inducing over-saving and under-consumption, was the direct source of unemployment and depressed trade. Protection by worsening the distribution of wealth must evidently aggravate this malady : more unearned income will accumulate as capital, seek investments in productive enterprises, stimulate business, congest markets, induce a slump of prices followed by a stoppage of production which will mean more unemployment of capital and labour. In other words, a protective system must aggravate under-consumption by increasing the proportion of the aggregate income of the community which goes to those who wish to apply much of that income to furthering more production and not to demanding consumable commodities, and by diminishing the proportion which goes to the classes which would use their incomes in raising their current standard of consumption.

§ 11. A protective system, then, far from furnishing a remedy, or even a genuine palliative, of unemployment, must exasperate the disease. Except in the peculiarly favoured industries for whose benefit the tariff is established, the rate of real wages and the volume of regular employment of labour must fall. Indeed, even in the favoured industries, though capital may be protected and able to earn higher profits, there is no reason to suppose that labour will earn any corresponding rise of wages. Almost the entire gain derived by agriculture from protection must pass to the landowner, the tenant-farmer benefiting only during the remainder of his lease ; though more agricultural labour might be employed, if a considerable import duty were imposed, the wages of that labour could not rise, or, if they rose for a short time, they must sink afterwards to conformity with the reduced standard of comfort of ordinary labour which we have seen to be a necessary result of protection. For no strong trade-union organisation is possible for agricultural labour, and any stimulus to agricultural employment, by checking the exodus from the country to the towns, and by calling back to the land rural labourers who had recently passed into the mining industry or into town work and who now suffered from the reactions of "protection" on these occupations, would adjust the supply of agricultural labour to the increased demand at a wage which, translated into purchasing power, would be lower than before. The same will hold of the protected manufactures; protection generates no economic force to enable the workers in these trades to share the gain of the employers, and where, as in the case of a few skilled, well-organised unions, they did stand to gain, this gain is purchased by a corresponding depression in general outside wages. In other words, there exists far more stability in protected land and protected capital than in protected labour; hence while the former can hold the subsidies which a tariff gives them, the latter cannot make good its claim to share the subsidies. It is easier for outside labour to enter the area of a protected industry than for outside capital. So even in the protected trades labour can have little hope of gain so far as wages are concerned; there will be more employment in these trades, a more than corresponding diminution of employment in other trades.

§ 12. Protectionism, thus interpreted, is one of the political defences instinctively thrown up by the proprietary classes against attacks upon their vested interests. The growing demand for equality of economic opportunities which, as education spreads, becomes a more definite and conscious policy in modern democracy, if it is to be effective, requires the cancelment of the advantages which scarcity of certain sorts of land, immobility of certain sorts of capital, restricted competition for certain sorts of highly remunerative and honourable employment, confer upon what, for convenience, we have termed the proprietary classes. These classes, when their privileges have been attacked, have always used in their defence whatever weapons political predominance placed in their hands.

Two closely co-operant weapons of defence are found in Imperial Expansion and Protection. The former appears at first sight to be distinctively political, the latter distinctively economic; in reality both represent the exploitation of political power by economic forces. Neither Imperialism nor Protectionism is, of course, a purely economic movement; in both instances the dominant directive economic interest utilises and assumes the protective colours of patriotism and humanitarian progress. The connection between the two consists in the fact that they both seek to achieve a readjustment between the political and the economic area of national life.

§ 13. The most important change in modern history has been the growing severance between the political and the industrial limits of national life; as a political unit a British citizen is confined in his interests to these isles, as an industrial unit he may be far more closely identified with China, South America, or Russia. The severance between political and industrial interests seems everywhere to threaten political solidarity, and sets up two tendencies, Imperialism and Protection. Imperialism represents a more or less conscious and organised effort of a nation to expand its old political boundaries, and to take in by annexation other outside countries where its citizens have acquired strong industrial interests. Protection represents the converse tendency, an effort to prevent industrial interests from wandering outside the political limits of the nation, to keep capital and labour employed within the political area, confining extra-national relations to commerce within the narrower limits of the term. Modern Conservatism, concerned for the territorial integrity of national life, pursues both policies, expanding political control, contracting industrial life, in order to try and preserve the identity of the politics and the industry of its citizens. It represents the struggle of a deformed and belated nationalism against the growing spirit which everywhere is breaking through the old national limits and is laying the economic foundation for the coming internationalism.

This is the inner meaning of the new wave of Protectionism in England. Its adherents fear lest England's natural advantages of soil, climate, position, labour-power, and business-enterprise should not suffice in the turmoil of keen world-competition to keep enough industry upon our national or imperial soil. The traditional policy of game-preserving impels them to have recourse to similar methods of preserving trade within the ring-fence of the national or imperial dominions.

Along with this sentiment works an allied sentiment of self-sufficiency. It is not enough that Great Britain should keep a large volume of industry within her shores ; she must defend herself against another implication of Free Trade, an excessive division of world-labour, which, by specialising the work of a nation, robs it of self-sufficiency. Even if Great Britain is strong enough to retain her fair share of world-industry, Free Trade, by confining British industry more and more to certain specific branches of manufacture and commerce, increases her dependence for the prime necessaries of national life upon the good-will and regular industry of other nations. When a nation depends for the supply of its daily bread upon the economic activity of other nations, its political independence is felt to be imperilled. Whatever be the advantage of international division of labour at ordinary times, it is felt that the national unit should, at any rate, not so far commit herself to specialised industry that she cannot, upon an emergency, resume the power to supply herself with food and other necessaries of life from her own resources.

Protectionism, interpreted in the light of these apprehensions, is an endeavour to struggle against certain dangers inherent in the world-economy of Free Trade, and to keep within the territorial limits of the nation a sufficient volume and an adequate variety of industry.

Now the free trader has several answers to this line of argument. Admitting that it is theoretically possible for trade to shrink in volume within the national area, as a result of free world-competition, he will deny that Great Britain is in fact subjected to this process. An impregnable array of evidence can be adduced to prove that our industrial prosperity is waxing, and not waning; that the diminution of certain old industries is attended by a more than proportionate growth of new industries; that the more rapid recent development of such countries as Germany and the United States is on the whole a source of strength, not of weakness, to our powers of national production; that certain particular injuries inflicted by the rivalry of nations are more than compensated by the indirect benefits of a more effective international co-operation. Every increase of the productive power of Germany and the United States is a source of increased wealth to Great Britain, just in proportion as the growing volume of our commerce with these countries obliges them to hand over to us, by ordinary processes of exchange, an increased quantity of their enhanced national wealth.

These commonplaces of the theory of free exchange are ignored by the fearful hosts of Protection.

As for the danger attributed to specialisation of industry which makes us dependent upon other nations for our food supply, the argument, so far as it carries any weight, relies on political rather than economic considerations. If there were any reason to expect a general conspiracy of foreign food-producing nations so blinded to their obvious self-interest as to establish a trade boycott against Great Britain, in such a case a policy of artificial stimulation of agriculture within the empire, though involving a great sacrifice of aggregate national wealth, would be defensible if it could be shown to be efficacious. But even here the Protectionist case collapses when from theory we resort to fact. For when we regard the amount of our dependence upon the United States and other foreign countries for our food and other necessaries of life, we shall perceive that we have gone too far in our international reliance for any such reversion to Imperial self-sufficiency to be efficacious. An endeavour to stimulate by artificial means the development of British and Imperial agriculture for purposes of self-support, while it would cost us dear, could not succeed within any reasonable time in securing us against the necessity of buying food from those foreign nations whom we are called upon to distrust. We should merely offend them without securing our economic independence. The politics of such a course would be even worse than its economics.

§ 14. But the deepest defect of the new Protectionism lies in its utter inadequacy to achieve its end. For if that end is to secure the retention of a sufficient volume and variety of industry and of industrial population within the territorial limits of the kingdom or the empire, the sort of protection which is now proposed will be quite incompetent to compass it.

This can easily be seen. The result of the specialisation of national industry under Free Trade (however imperfect or "one-sided") is to enhance the productivity of the capital and labour engaged in it. An artificial restriction of this process of specialisation must therefore be attended by a diminution of the general productivity of capital and labour. The instructed Protectionist will hardly question this. Either he will admit a reduction of aggregate national wealth, defending it on the ground of greater variety and increased self-sufficiency; or he will assert that a larger employment of capital and labour will enable the same quantity of wealth to be produced as before. It matters not which line of argument is taken, the fact remains that the result of Protection will be a diminished productivity of capital and labour *per unit*. This must be attended by a general shrinkage in the rate of profits and of wages, a process accelerated by the fact that rent of land will take a larger share of the total diminished national income. Now, if profits and wages fall, both capital and labour will tend to seek employment outside the protected area, in foreign lands; the fact that protective systems prevail in these foreign lands, not being a new factor in the situation, is immaterial. So, even if it be argued that an increased volume of employment of capital and labour might directly ensue from a protective tariff, that capital and labour, obtaining a lower rate of real remuneration, will not stay within the protected national area, but will tend to seek the more remunerative outside employment. This theory is supported by innumerable concrete evidences.

Protection, by lowering the average productiveness of capital and labour, tends to expel them from the protected area. Capital, more fluid, leaves more easily and quickly; labour lags, and a grave condition of "unemployment" embarrasses the situation; eventually labour too migrates in order to co-operate with its necessary economic adjunct. Can Protection stop this process of migration which plainly defeats its end by exasperating the very disease it is designed to cure? Yes, provided it is sufficiently thorough. Protection, to be effective, must not stand upon the feeble expedients of preferential or even prohibitive

N

tariffs aimed against the import of foreign goods. It must support this barrier by a second barrier, prohibiting the export of British capital and British labour. The more rigorous Protection of the seventeenth and eighteenth centuries took what steps in this direction were then necessary, by restriction or prohibition of the export of machinery and skilled labour. More rigorous protective measures would now be needed. For the fluidity of the monetary investments in foreign lands was then a *négligeable* factor : whereas it is the factor of first significance in modern world industry. In order then for our new Protectionists to gain their object of setting back the tide of industrial internationalism, so as to achieve the economic solidarity and self-sufficiency of the British Empire, they must devise means of preventing fluid capital and labour from leaving the country. Unless they see their way to carry Protection thus far, they will behold their policy of protective and retaliatory tariffs reduced to nullity by the free play of the enlightened self-interest of capital and labour seeking elsewhere the employment now rendered unprofitable within the British Empire.

Nothing short of this protective policy of "thorough," making for the well-nigh complete economic isolation of our empire, by a virtual prohibition, not only of imports but of exports, can avail to safeguard the nation against the imaginary perils of a free-trade economy which is only the

industrial aspect of the slowly growing internationalism with which lies the future of civilisation.

§ 15. Protectionism, thus interpreted, is the ex-
pression of a spurious patriotism seeking to confine
industry within a national or imperial area, so as to
defend the nation, or the empire, against what it
regards as the disintegrating influences of commercial
internationalism.

Now this patriotism is doubly false as expressed
in that form of preferential Protectionism now before
our country. In the first place, if carried into effect,
it would injure our national life by narrowing the
stream of intercourse with other nations, upon which
in the future, as in the past, the growth and enrich-
ment of our nationality depend. It is no better for
a nation than for a man to live alone, and the
economic self-sufficiency at which Protection aims,
could it be achieved, would deprive our national
industry and our national life of those new supplies
of foreign stock and stimuli which have played so
large a part in building the very industries which we
have come to regard as characteristically British.
The greatness of English manufacture and commerce
is so demonstrably due to the free receptivity of
England; so many of her industries are the direct
product of Flemish, Italian, French and German skill
and invention, drawn into our country by our industrial and political practice of the open door, that any
stoppage of this liberty of foreign access, such as

must attend any substantial measure of Protectionism, would inflict the gravest damage upon a main source of our national industrial growth. Even more detrimental would be the diminution of all forms of higher intercourse which this lessening of commercial intercourse must involve. Ideas always follow trade routes, and a limitation of international trade will restrict the free flow of ideas and feelings between Great Britain and foreign nations, and will throw us more and more upon the restricted intellectual resources of our empire. It is not extravagant to suggest that we have more to learn from France, Germany, and America than from Australasia and South Africa; and that if it were a case of making immediate economic sacrifices, it would pay us better as a nation in the long run to maintain a free expansive intercourse with foreign civilised nations than to cultivate a process of narrow, intellectual inbreeding within the British Empire. As matters stand, our immediate economic interests are so plainly identical with the wider, higher interests of our national civilisation that the proposed change of commercial policy would inflict a double blow upon our national life.

§ 16. Protectionism, then, thus regarded is a disinterested but mistaken form of patriotism. But this disinterested popular spirit is directed by more definitely economic interests which utilise it for their defence and profit. Protection, like Imperial Expansion, is of double service to the vested interests. On the one hand, just as Imperial Expansion ripens and improves their private foreign investments at the public expense and furnishes through the rising national expenditure a profitable market for their goods and services, so Protection enables them at once to increase their rents and profits at the expense of the main body of producers and consumers and to consolidate their capitalist structure so as better to repress competition and control their market. On the other hand, Protection, like Imperial Expansion, by rousing feelings of antagonism against foreign nations, and representing the commercial co-operation of the industrial world as a rivalry of nations in the struggle for a limited amount of market, succeeds in diverting into external channels the stream of reform energy which surges up in the life of nations.

Protection, like Imperialism, is a class policy, instinctively devised in order to break and divide, and so to render impotent, the blind, ill-directed forces of social reform which are groping after the establishment of a juster economic order that will secure a more equitable distribution of wealth by an equalisation of economic opportunities. Such an analysis does not impute base motives, as may at first sight appear. Of the driving forces in history but a very small proportion enter the restricted area of clear consciousness and are fully recognised as motives. But when we analyse the actual path taken by a "movement" and find that in all its turns it subserves the actual interests of certain groups or classes of men, we are justified in concluding that these interests constitute the real motive of the movement.

In that sense, and in that sense alone, does Protection rank as one of the aggressive and defensive policies of a proprietary class or group of classes seeking to make positive gains for themselves out of the loss of their fellow-citizens and to defend against popular assaults the economic and political powers which enable them to make these gains.

CHAPTER XII

PROTECTION AND SOCIALISM

§ 1

OUR analysis of the conditions under which exchange of commodities or services takes place, either between members of the same nation or members of different nations, discloses the absence of that complete equality of economic opportunity essential to full freedom of exchange. Obstacles to mobility of the factors of production are everywhere forming bases of "scarcity" values which sometimes change the structure of a competitive market into a qualified or an absolute monopoly. The superior bargaining power thus vested in certain buyers or sellers is liable to become so oppressive and injurious either to the general public or to some class as to evoke legislative interference in restraint of "free" contracts between parties so unequally equipped. Poverty or ignorance may deprive a person of true liberty of contract; he may not know the nature of the bargain he enters, or knowing it he may be unable to refuse to enter it; or else the contract may be made for him to his detriment by a parent or other person claiming to act on his behalf; or finally, the contract, though entered with equal liberty and knowledge by both parties, may be so injurious to the family or to other members of society as to be adjudged contrary to public policy.

These are some grounds upon which legislative interference with freedom of economic contract has taken place in civilised communities. All such legislation may be regarded as "protective" and as involving a formal restraint of "free exchange." In most instances the "freedom" which is interfered with is unsubstantial. The coercion and protection of factory, public health, and other legislative interference with "freedom" of the sale of labour-power is a recognition of the inability of workers in many industries to bargain effectively regarding hours of labour, sanitation, security against accidents, etc., with their employers. In the case of children and many young persons there can be no serious pretence that they are "free agents." In the case of many classes of adult workers, especially women, the limitations of their choice with regard to kind and terms of employment are such as leave them little real liberty; they must effect a continuous sale of the only thing they have to offer in exchange, their labour-power; they must sell in a particular locality upon terms regarding price, hours, etc., which, as individuals, they are powerless to modify and cannot reject. The largest infringement of a pure policy of *laissez-faire* in the determination of sales consists in this regulation of the sale of labour-power. Drastic measures of " protection " are enforced in connection with the sale of professional services, designed partly to secure "fair remuneration " for the profession, partly to protect the " consumer," whose "liberty" in buying professional services is impaired by necessary ignorance. Partly, again, as a protection of the consumer, partly as an act of public policy, certain material commodities are removed from a " free market " and can be sold only in licensed places or by licensed persons under rigorous conditions : alcoholic liquor and drugs are chief instances. Various laws protect the consumer against poisonous or adulterated articles; others deal with misdescription of kind, quality, or origin.

§ 2. This legislative interference, though chiefly directed to processes of production, involves a considerable restraint of " freedom of exchange " in internal trade. To some the regulation of external trade appears a natural extension or corollary of this regulation of internal trade. Certain contracts or other bargains are removed from the legitimate area of " free exchange " in domestic trade, may not certain bargains be similarly restrained in foreign trade?

The issue is sometimes put from the standpoint of capital claiming " protection " against foreign competition as a counter-weight to the "protection" afforded to labour by factory acts and other "social" legislation. The effect of this legislative "protection" of labour, it is urged, is to raise the expenses of production in this country as compared with other countries, and so to expose our markets to the invasion of foreign goods which can undersell our goods, because they are produced without such expensive restrictions.

The "labour" in trades closely pressed by foreign competition sometimes, identifying its cause with that of "capital," presses the same argument, protesting against the goods it produces being undersold by the products of "sweated" labour abroad. "Why," it is asked, "should we permit our trades to be thus handicapped in our own markets; surely we ought to impose the same restraints on foreign goods which we impose upon our own goods? You try to stop Germans from producing 'sweated' clothes in London and selling them, why allow them to make the same clothes in Hamburg and send them over to sell at the same price in our market?"

It is not always clearly seen that these cases involve the entire policy of free imports. Are we to stop the entrance of German hardware, which may be able to undersell our goods, on account of the low wages and long hours of German labour, while we continue to give free admission to American hardware which may undersell our goods by reason of the better machinery and methods or the greater intensity of labour in the American shops? The American underselling would harm our industry just as much as the German underselling; shall we be guided by cosmopolitan philanthropy to discriminate against the German, imposing duties in order to teach the German Government its duties to German labour?

In fact, the policy would be more difficult than this. We should find that American mills were underselling us, partly by using better machinery and method, partly by working longer hours and securing greater intensity of labour; in other words, by "sweating." Could we distinguish how much was due to one, how much to the other cause? Proceeding further, we should find that almost every country from which goods entered our ports to compete with our own products had lower rates of wages and longer hours, etc., than prevailed in Great Britain; if we apply our standard of wages and hours, all foreign goods are sweated; if we do not apply our standard, what other standard is justified by the logic of protection of labour?

The notion of a "scientific tariff" directed to equalise the cost of labour in foreign countries with our own by imposing import duties equivalent to the lower foreign costs, though taken as the formal basis of tariff policy in America, has never been seriously applied, and is incapable of application. It would involve, if logically carried out, an absolute prohibition of all foreign competition on the part of the nations furthest advanced in conditions of labour. In practice it would require an impossibly accurate knowledge of the ever-changing conditions of all parts of the various trades in different nations of the world, and a continual readjustment of import duties, to accord with the changes. Nothing short of this could be designated a scientific tariff for protection.

"Sweating" and "unfair trading" are difficult terms to define when exclusive regard is paid to internal industry. How impossible, if they involved a detailed comparison of the standard of life and the methods of production in the case respectively of the United States, Germany, China, and West Africa!

§ 3. There are two plain reasons why a protective tariff imposed on "sweated" or cheaply produced foreign goods is no true pendant or supplement to the industrial legislation in "protection" of labour in home industries.

The first is that it is not in accordance with our national interest to stop cheap goods from coming into this country, when that cheapness is durable; the second is that we have no duty and no power to control the legislation affecting the conditions of production in foreign countries.

To the first reason it may, perhaps, be objected: "But the importation of sweated goods affects injuriously our nation regarded as 'producers.'" The answer here is a flat denial. The irregular or casual dumping of such goods does injure certain British trades, and it has been admitted that, under certain circumstances, protection might be applicable, if it could be properly safeguarded. But the regular admission of foreign goods which, whether products of a sweating system or of superior technical economies, undersell our goods in our own market, is a benefit and not an injury to British industry. It is to the real advantage of the British nation, not merely in its capacity of consumers, but of producers, to permit freely the displacement of the capital and labour in a trade which can be systematically undersold by foreign goods ; the temporary loss and waste will be more than compensated by the diversion of industrial energy to other employments. The fact that this argument fails to convince the practical man is due to the absence of any governmental policy of compensation for the capital and labour thus displaced and cancelled in the interest of the larger public. Such compensation for displacement is a logical implication of a sound social policy. So far as capital is concerned, it would be very difficult of application ; so far as labour is concerned, it forms a powerful basis of appeal for a scheme of public relief for "the unemployed," not as a charitable measure, but as a plain demand of social justice and public expediency. The failure of Government hitherto to recognise adequately this duty of easing industrial displacements of capital and labour, desirable in the general interest of commerce, must not drive us to the expedient of an artificial prevention of these displacements, which are the very conditions of progress in our industrial life. If every British trade in danger of being undersold by foreigners in the home market could call upon our Government to stop that competition (for this is what protection against foreign sweated goods signifies), industry would *pro tanto* be stereotyped in this country, and progress, alike in methods of production and in selection of employment for capital and labour, would be grievously impaired. So much for the first point. The regular admission of "sweated goods" from foreign countries is not detrimental but beneficial to British industry.

§ 4. Now, in answer to the second objection, we should urge that our legislative interference with conditions of production in British industries is not designed to prevent goods from being sold cheap, though it may have that effect, but to safeguard the welfare of certain classes of labour in the interest of the nation. It is part of the duty of our Government as representing the nation to insist that the conditions of production in this country shall conform to a certain standard of security and decency. We have no corresponding duty with regard to processes of production in other countries, nor have we any power of undertaking such a task; we have no machinery for the ascertainment or the repression of foreign "sweating." A purely national legislative body is competent to deal with "sweating" and with other conditions of industry within the nation ; it is not competent to deal with foreign sweating. If there existed an international legislature, it might fitly deal with it. Each nation can only insist that the industries conducted within its area shall be sanitary and otherwise socially sound ; it is brought into contact, not with the production, but only with the products of foreign industry, and the fact that such products are cheap when they reach our consumers is regarded by our Government as a good and not an evil to our nation, which wants to consume them or to utilise them for further production.

It is open to any private association of British citizens, such as a trade union, recognising the international solidarity of the interests of labour, to support a strike instituted by foreign workers to put down "sweating" or otherwise to improve their condition, but such an association cannot legitimately call upon the British Government to assist them by tariff legislation. It is, of course, true that free importation of foreign goods makes it more difficult for trade-union action to secure conditions of labour entailing higher expenses of production than are incurred by foreign competition, and our Government is naturally influenced by such considerations in devising further expensive restrictions upon

British trades exposed to such competition. The proper method of dealing with this difficulty, however, is not by a tariff war, but by attempts at organising international agreement. Industrial legislation along the same general lines is a common policy of all modern civilised states. Conferences and informal agreements as to pace and methods of labour legislation have already been established; further progress along this road to political internationalism of a real though limited kind may be expected. Nothing short of international government can serve to exercise over inequalities of international exchange a control corresponding to that which a national government can exercise over inequalities of internal exchange.

§ 5. Protective tariffs are in no sense a counterpart of legislation in "protection" of the interests of labour. They do not even protect capital as a whole, but only certain sorts of capital at the expense of other sorts of capital and of the general industrial interests of the country. They also protect certain sorts of labour, though far less effectively, as we have seen. Whereas the essence of sound industrial legislation is a restraint of unfree competition and unequal bargaining in the exchange of goods and services, the essence of protective tariffs is to bestow privilege upon those very interests which are already strongest in their powers of advantageous exchange of the goods and services they sell, *i.e.* the landowners and the better-organised, wealthier, and more influential capitalists in manufacture and in commerce.

Inequalities exist in the processes of exchange between members of different nations, though not so large, so numerous, or so complex as in the processes of domestic exchange. But while national legislation may by judicious restraints do something to redress or mitigate the latter, it cannot, save in rarely exceptional cases, do anything to redress or mitigate the former. For in the one case both parties to the act of exchange and the entire process of exchange are within the jurisdiction of the national government, in the other case only one of the parties and one end of the process of exchange.

§6. Thus the claim sometimes advanced on behalf of Protection that it can serve the interests of the general body of producers in a nation by securing them against an injurious competition of foreigners is perceived to be fallacious. It can only set up privileged classes of producers at the expense of the other producers of the nation. This fundamental truth is sometimes obscured by a false antithesis between producer and consumer. Free imports are represented as a consumer's policy; Protection as a producer's policy. Although this fallacy has already been unmasked by our proof that Protection cannot increase the volume of employment of the factors of production, it deserves further attention on account of the superficial support given to it by the universally

o

accepted habit of distinguishing producer and consumer in discussing the incidence of taxation. For convenience we say the producer pays this duty, the consumer that, or that they each pay a proportion of the duty; and in dealing with tariffs on foreign trade which have regard to what are in effect halves of acts of international exchange, it is not improper to mark this distinction. But in any close scrutiny into real incidence of taxation the antithesis of producer and consumer disappears; the latter has no rightful place. In the distribution of wealth there is no consumer, unless that title be reserved for pensioners and other receivers of fixed incomes. With the exception of this abnormal class, all incomes are paid to the owners of a factor of production for the use of the factor which they own. The true incidence of every tax is its effect upon the real income received as rent by landowners, as interest by capitalists, as profit or salaries by employers, as the fees by professional men, and as wages by employees. When we say that a duty falls on the consumer, we simply mean that the price of a commodity has risen, and that those who buy it are *primâ facie* injured in their real income, which is reduced in its purchasing power. But this is only the beginning of the analysis of incidence. The real incomes thus assailed have more or less power of resistance; the attempt embodied in the tax to reduce the real payment received for the service of a factor of production is only fully successful when the factor yields a scarcity rent or other surplus income which is not a payment necessary to induce the owner of the factor to employ it. The landowner who receives economic rent cannot recoup himself for a rise in prices of commodities by raising his rent, and the recipient of high dividends from a manufacturing monopoly cannot raise the prices of the goods he sells, which are *ex hypothesi* already fixed so as to yield the maximum net return on the business.

But where incomes are determined by normal competitive conditions the attempt of a tax to reduce real incomes will not be equally successful. Capitalists, professional men, and wage-earners, receiving payments which are what they regard as minimum profits or subsistence wages, will in some cases refuse the use of their factor of production for a lower real payment than before, and this reduction in the supply of certain sorts of capital, skill, or labour will cause a rise of the price so as to maintain the former rate of real payment, and to throw the onus of the duty upon some other class. More simply stated, the incidence of a tax falling in the first instance on the consumer is an attempt to reduce his customary standard of comfort ; this he will resist so far as he can by raising the price of the factor of production which furnishes his livelihood. Every class whose remuneration is competitively determined has some power of resisting an attack upon the standard of comfort by throwing upon other classes the burden of a tax directed at it. But that power of resistance differs widely in different classes, and depends upon a great variety of special circumstances : upon the stability which habit has given to a standard of consumption ; upon the effect of a reduction of consumption upon efficiency of labour ; upon the strength of organisation of a trade or a profession ; upon the ability of individuals to refuse to sell their factor of production for a lower real payment.   Each of these circumstances opens up a very intricate series of considerations, each of which would require to be considered both by itself and in its relation to other circumstances before we could form any reasonable judgment of the probable effects of (say) a tax on grain raising the price of bread 10 per cent. upon the real income of any single class or trade in the nation.   Such an investigation would require answers to be given to a series of important and difficult questions such as the following : What proportion of the income of such a class is expended in the purchase of bread ?   How far could and would some other form of food, not proportionately raised in price, be substituted for bread ? What effect, if any, would a reduced consumption of bread, or of some other commodity, less of which is now purchased in order to buy more bread, have upon the efficiency and wage-earning power of the chief wage-earner and the supplementary wage-earners respectively ?   How far is it possible for such wage-earners by individual or collective bargaining to squeeze out of the profits of the trade at which they work a higher money wage to enable them to pay for dearer bread? If combined pressure forced employers to pay higher wages in such a trade, could they, the employers, throw any considerable part of the burden on landlords in reduced rent, or on the consuming public in enhanced prices of the goods they make?

None of these leading questions could be answered without opening up a series of further questions. Indeed, the last—and perhaps the most important— the question whether increased wages could be squeezed out of a trade by raising prices, obviously involves a repetition of the same circle of questions in relation to each class of consumers upon which our first class proposes to shift its burden.

No attempt can here be made towards a practical solution of the question who will really pay, when a tax is said to fall on the consumer. It would, in fact, be necessary to enter into a most minute investigation of the conditions of the trade or occupation from which each consumer drew his income in order to ascertain how far he ultimately bore the tax which raised the price of the commodities he consumed.

Not less intricate would be the scientific analysis of the incidence of a tax which fell in the first instance on a particular class of producers, thus affecting the expenses of production of a particular class of commodities. Here, too, it is a question of relative resistance and transferability.

§ 7. We may summarise the theory of the case as follows: A protective system does not "protect" the producers of the nation which imposes it; it "protects" certain privileged classes at the expense, not ultimately of the consumer, but of other classes of producers. It injures the body of producers in two ways: first, by causing an artificial misapplication of productive energy, which reduces the total productivity of national wealth for exchange and consumption; secondly, by enabling these privileged producers to tax the other producers of the nation which has imposed the tariff, each class of producer suffering in proportion to its inability to shift on to other classes the portion of the tax which falls upon it in a reduction of the purchasing power of the income it receives for the use of its factor of production.

INDEX

www.ingramcontent.com/pod-product-compliance
Lightning Source LLC
Chambersburg PA
CBHW020532270326
41927CB00006B/545